D0048132

How to be a
Successful
Teenager

18 SECRETS EVERY TEEN
MUST KNOW TO SUCCEED

Rick Jones

CHICK PUBLICATIONS
ONTARIO, CALIFORNIA

Published by:
    CHICK PUBLICATIONS
    PO Box 3500, Ontario, Calif. 91761-1019 USA
    Tel: (909) 987-0771
    Fax: (909) 941-8128
    Web: www.chick.com/es
    Email: postmaster@chick.com

Printed in the United States of America

ISBN: 978-0-9379-5844-5

Library of Congress Catalog Card Number: 94-92412

Contents

Mary Anne wasn't planning on dying!

After all, she was only 13 years old. But when she called two boys she had dated and announced that she was pregnant, that's exactly what happened.

The startled boys loaded two .22 caliber rifles and headed for Mary Anne's house. They picked the seventh grader up and drove her to an isolated field.

Once there, they blindfolded her, forced her to strip to her underwear, and gave her a stuffed dog to hold. They then stood her against a tree to be executed. The coroner later reported that she was shot seven times.

But this gruesome and senseless murder became even more tragic when an autopsy showed that Mary Anne wasn't pregnant after all.

WHY THE DESTRUCTION?

Why are the lives of so many young people being shattered? In working with teenagers, I've learned that it's usually because they never learned the 18 secrets this world system is purposely keeping from them.

And just because a teen claims to be a Christian doesn't mean he or she is immune. Tragically, statistics show that Christian teens are now being devoured just as rapidly as their non-Christian peers.

Experts claim that Christian young people are even *committing suicide* at the same rate as non-Christian teens.[1] Therefore, *all* teenagers need to learn what's being kept from them, no matter what their religious beliefs.

I've seen miraculous changes take place in the lives of young people who discovered these secrets. Their feelings of hopelessness and despair were replaced by joy and contentment.

Teen, you have an enemy who does **NOT** want you to learn the truth because he knows it can revolutionize your life. He wants to keep you in the dark so he can make you his next victim.

This book was written to uncover these well-kept secrets, so you can experience real peace and freedom in your life.

Please don't let anyone or anything stop you from reading this book. After years of watching young lives being needlessly snuffed out, my desire is that you will read... believe... and escape the deadly snares that are being laid for you.

If your life is going great, these truths can help keep you headed in the right direction. If you are suffering, or if you've ever thought about taking your life... before you do anything, please read this book.

If you are unhappy, your life can change! There *are* answers for your problems, no matter how hopeless your situation may seem. If you're tired of life the way it is now, it *can* change...

starting right now!

1

You Are In A War...
Right Now!

**"I can't take it anymore! I feel like
I'm being ripped apart inside!"**

Steve is tormented by thoughts like these quite
often.

On the outside, he may appear to have his life
together, but on the inside, he feels like an
overheated radiator on a 110 degree summer
day—ready to explode!

His parents think that he is a fairly happy
Christian young man, but in reality, he feels
like he's being pulled in a thousands directions.

His parents are under the impression that he

has adopted all of their beliefs, but he hasn't. They have no idea how much peer pressure he faces, even though he attends a Christian school.

He wants to remain pure sexually, but all his friends are pressuring him to have sex, and he knows that his girlfriend is willing. But he is scared to death about sexually transmitted diseases, getting his girlfriend pregnant, and mostly AIDS.

"NOBODY KNOWS HOW I FEEL!"

His parents don't like his music, his friends or his grades. They nag at him about the value of going to college but he's not sure he wants to. But, then again, he doesn't know what he does want to do.

Life is easier when he's with his friends. Or is it? They heap just as much pressure on him as his parents. They just pressure him to do different things.

Drugs are everywhere and he wonders if he should try them. His parents don't know it, but a kid at school is a dealer and will sell him anything he wants.

Then Steve wonders about the future. Will the world survive? Should I live it up now and take my chances? Or should I work hard and plan for the future?

Though he's never said a word about it to

anyone, he sometimes lays in bed at night and thinks about ending it all.

He's too ashamed to confess his feelings to his parents, his pastor, or anyone else. So he holds them all inside and tries to deal with them as best he can.

He hears many conflicting messages. Movies, TV, and his friends pull him one way. Church and the Bible pull him another. His mind is usually swimming. Which way should I go? Who should I listen to? He feels bombarded from all sides... like he's in the middle of an intense war.

WHAT ABOUT YOU?

Have you ever had any of these feelings, young person? Have you ever felt like your life was a literal war zone, and you were out there on the front lines. If so, there is an excellent reason why...

BECAUSE YOU ARE IN A WAR!

It's no accident that the lives of hundreds of thousands of teens are ravaged every year. They are casualties of war. But it's not a physical war, it's a spiritual war.

All around you, an unseen spiritual war is raging. And at the forefront of this battle to destroy you is your worst enemy, an enemy you may not even know you have.

And until your spiritual eyes are opened and

you understand this first secret, you don't have a chance of surviving his deadly attacks.

THE DECEIVER

Who is this enemy that is trying to destroy you? His name is Satan. And he wants to see you suffer while you're alive—and burn in hell for the rest of eternity.

You may think this is a big joke right now, but you won't after you breathe your last breath, and the flames of hell begin engulfing your body.

And even if you don't know it, God, in His love, warned you about this enemy a long time ago:

> "Be sober, be vigilant; because your adversary (enemy) the devil, as a roaring lion, walketh about, *seeking whom he may devour."* 1 Peter 5:8

If you are snickering in disbelief, you have been terribly deceived and are already under the control of this enemy. Please keep reading so you can learn how to break free of his grasp.

Young person, whether you know it or not, right now, your enemy, Satan, is pounding on you from every side. And he's gearing up for his knockout punch:

> "For we wrestle not against flesh and blood, but against principalities, against powers, against the rulers of the darkness of this world, *against*

> *spiritual wickedness in high places."*
> Ephesians 6:12

You may think that your problem is your mom, your dad, your boyfriend or girlfriend, or others, but they're not. Satan often uses people (knowingly or unknowingly) to hurt you, but people are **NOT** your problem.

Your real problem is Satan and his unseen demonic forces, who are working hard to ruin your life.

If you don't know this, you make your enemy's job a lot easier. He has a much easier time destroying those who never learn this secret.

"I THINK I'LL KILL MYSELF"

A 16-year-old boy concluded that life was no longer worth living, so he closed himself in his bedroom, raised a gun barrel to his head and pulled the trigger. His mother found his dead body sprawled in a pool of blood with a bullet through his brain.

What horrible tragedy made this boy feel he had no alternative but to kill himself? His suicide note told the answer:

> "Mom, I have nothing else to live for. Nobody loves me. My favorite band has just broke up, and now I have nothing to live for, so I'm going to kill myself and go to hell, cause I know the devil loves me."[1]

How sad! This deceived young man died in combat. He was another casualty of war... a war he didn't even know he was in.

If you were cruising down the street and a friend went flying past you in his car, then later bragged to everyone that he beat you in a race, you'd argue, "I didn't have a chance. I didn't even know I was in a race."

In the same way, you don't stand a chance against Satan unless you first recognize that you are in a spiritual war.

This young man didn't know about the spiritual war, so he tried to solve his problems by killing himself and going to hell because, "I know the devil loves me."

Where do you suppose he got that lie? The devil deceived him, then persuaded him to take his own life. Now he'll pay the price for that mistake forever in a lake of fire.

"WHY CAN'T I CHANGE?"

At some point in their descent to destruction, many teens reach a point where they say:

> "I've had enough. It's time to get my life together."

They decide to begin solving their problems. This is when they make a shocking discovery...

THEY CAN'T DO IT!

No matter how much effort they put forth, they

can't fix the problems that plague them. In fact, teens often say, "The harder I try, the worse things get!"

The reason they couldn't fix their problems was because their problems weren't physical, they were spiritual. And nobody can fix spiritual problems on their own. You must have God's help. Jesus said:

"...without me ye can do *nothing.*"
John 15:5

TERRY'S DILEMMA

Terry was a 15-year-old girl who wanted to do right. But each time she attempted to take one step forward, she fell two steps back.

When life became unbearable at home, she ran away, thinking a new location would solve her problems. But it didn't. In fact, the harder she tried to make life better, the uglier it grew. Terry finally realized that she couldn't help herself.

Terry needed to learn that she was in a spiritual war and that her problems weren't physical, they were spiritual. And you can never win spiritual battles using physical weapons.

Once Terry learned that she was in a spiritual war, all her tactics changed. Instead of trying to solve physical problems, she began solving her spiritual problems.

Within a few weeks, Terry's life was totally

transformed. Joy radiated from her face. Contentment filled her heart. The change in her life was dramatic. What happened? Terry learned the first secret to having a happy and successful life.

THE FIRST SECRET

The first secret Satan has been keeping from you is that you are in a spiritual war. Here's the simple truth in a nutshell. God loves you and wants to bless you and give you joy.

The devil, on the other hand, hates you and wants to curse and ravage your life. Both God and Satan are well aware that you are in a war and both have developed a war plan they would like you to follow.

GOD'S WAR PLAN

God wants to give you a wonderful victory in this war. He longs to bless and protect you. He has given you hundreds of great promises in His Word, the Bible. Here's one:

> "For the Lord God is a sun and shield: the Lord will give grace and glory: ***no good thing will he withold from them that walk uprightly.***"   Psalm 84:11

Then after you die, God's desire is that you will enjoy paradise in Heaven with Him:

> "The Lord is... not willing that ***any*** should perish, but that ***all*** should come to repentance.   2 Peter 3:9

Right now, God Almighty is reaching out to you in love, asking you to forsake the devil and turn to Him, so you can be victorious in this brutal war and enjoy the peace that only Jesus can give.

SATAN'S WAR PLAN

The devil's plan is to fill your life with as much torment and agony as possible. He specializes in dishing out pain, suffering, heartache and misery. What makes him especially dangerous is that, to lure teens into his traps, he uses bait that is very appealing to teens, like sex, drugs, rock music, etc.

The devil's ultimate goal is to deceive everyone he can into following him into the lake of fire, where he knows *he* will spend eternity:

> "And the devil that deceived them was *cast into the lake of fire and brimstone..."*   Revelation 20:10

If you don't discover and accept God's one and only way to heaven before you die, you will hear God say these awful words to you when you die:

> "Depart from me, ye cursed, into ever-lasting fire, prepared for the devil and his angels."   Matthew 25:41

To lead you straight down the path to eternal destruction, Satan must make sure that you never learn that you are in a spiritual war.

Those are the two sides. And there you are, right in the middle of this fierce spiritual war. If you think that you are exempt from Satan's devices because you are a Christian, you are wrong. The devil is probably working on you twice as hard.

Teen, God is reaching out to you. He wants to open your eyes so you can see what's really going on. But at the same time, Satan is clawing at you for all he's worth, trying to keep you ignorant, so he can destroy you.

No wonder you have so many problems. No wonder you usually feel like you're under attack... **YOU ARE!**

YOU'RE ON YOUR WAY

Now you know the first secret... and that's the first step to victory. By the time you finish this book, you'll know 17 more of the devil's best-kept battle secrets... secrets that open doors to happiness, peace and success.

Don't let the devil keep slicing you to pieces, while hiding quietly in the shadows. You know his first secret. Keep reading and see what other truths he's keeping from you...

2

The Secret About Hell

It was a gruesome sight!

When Bill arrived, there had obviously been a horrible accident. A severely smashed car was laying upside down in the middle of the road.

As Bill approached, he saw Susan, a teenage girl, trapped inside, furiously pounding on the window and screaming for help.

Just as Bill reached her car, it exploded in flames, knocking him backwards. As the flames engulfed Susan, Bill found a large rock and quickly smashed the windshield. He grabbed Susan's burning body and dragged her to safety.

As he rolled Susan in some nearby grass to extinguish the flames, the stench of her burning flesh almost caused him to pass out. She was burned over most of her body and was screaming in agony.

AN ETERNAL FIRE

Teen, as ghastly as that story is, it does not begin to describe the horrors of a real place that real people are sent to every day.

The place is hell. It's a place of eternal torment where people burn day and night forever and ever in undying flames.

Susan suffered excruciating pain and horrible burns but at least she escaped with her life.

In hell, there is no escape—*ever!* And there is no hope. For all eternity, every person in hell will scream in horror as roaring flames engulf their body, just like Susan did when she was burning. And it doesn't matter what you believe about hell:

- It doesn't matter if you don't believe hell exists—it does.

- It doesn't matter if you believe that a loving God would never send anyone to such a place—He does.

- It doesn't matter if you think I am trying to scare you into believing God and doing what He wants you to do—I'm not.

I am only telling you the truth so you'll know the consequences of following Satan instead of God.

Unfortunately, Satan has done an excellent job of brainwashing people into believing that hell is something other than what it really is.

Have you ever heard... or worse... believed one of these statements, young person?

- **Hell is going to be one big party!**
- **All my friends will be there!**
- **If my rock star idols are going to hell, I want to go there too!**
- **In hell, I'll have ultimate power!**

If you have, the truth about hell is going to be a shocker for you. Satan has convinced many young people that hell "ain't a bad place to be." Many of the devil's most powerful ministers are preaching this message. Here are a few of their most popular sermons:

"Hell Ain't A Bad Place To Be" - AC/DC

> "Round my heart. Tear it apart
> You got the Devil and me.
> Hell ain't a bad place to be
> Oh I said, Hell ain't a bad place to be.
> Oh no, Hell ain't a bad place to be..."

Here is another example:

"To Hell And Back" - Venom

> "You can take a trip with me

> Hell's my final home
> If you wish to live with night
> Watch the demons roam
> Holding high the Southern Cross
> Watch the mortals blaze
> Drink the blood and feel my wrath
> To Hell and back..."

As a result of all this "advertising," many teens don't fear going to hell. In fact, some are even looking forward to it. Remember the deceived young man in chapter one, who said:

> "... I have nothing to live for, so I'm going to kill myself **and go to hell, cause I know the devil loves me.**"

You need to understand that Satan is the biggest liar who has ever lived. The Bible says that he is the father of liars:

> "When he (Satan) speaketh a lie, he speaketh of his own: **for he is a liar, and the father of it.**"   John 8:44

Those who tell you that hell "ain't a bad place to be" are servants of Satan—and they're lying, like their father, Satan, taught them to.

If you wait until after you die to learn this fact, there will be no escape. You'll know you were deceived, but you will burn forever.

Hell will NOT be a party!

Hell is the most horrible place of punishment ever created. It is a terrifying place, worse than anything you can imagine. It is reserved for Satan and those who choose to follow him!

Obviously, Satan does not want anyone to learn this secret because it's sure to turn any thinking person away from following him.

THE TRUTH

Please open your eyes and discover this truth now, before you face those awful consequences. God has spelled it out for you in His Word, and His Word is truth:

> "Sanctify them through thy truth: thy word (the Bible) *is truth.*"
> John 17:17

You've listened to the lies of the devil and his servants long enough. Please open your ears to the truth. The very reason people are condemned to hell is because they rejected the wonderful truths in God's Word:

> "That they all might be damned *who believed not the truth,* but had pleasure in unrighteousness."
> 2 Thessalonians 2:12

WHAT HELL IS REALLY LIKE

Since all eternity rests upon what you decide, please consider carefully the following:

> "And the devil that deceived them was cast into the *lake of fire and brimstone*, where the beast and

the false prophet are, and shall be tormented day and night for ever and ever." Revelation 20:10

Remember teen, these are not my words or my opinions. These are God's Words and this is what God is saying to **you:**

"And these shall go away into **everlasting punishment:** but the righteous into life eternal."
Matthew 25:46

"But the children of the kingdom shall be cast out into **outer darkness:** there shall be **weeping and gnashing of teeth.**" Matthew 8:12

Are you getting the picture? Hell is definitely **NOT** a party. It's a horrible place of eternal punishment for those who follow Satan:

"Who shall be punished with **everlasting destruction** from the presence of the Lord, and from the glory of his power:"
2 Thessalonians 1:9

Because it is so important, God warns us over and over how awful hell is:

"...he (those who follow Satan) shall be **tormented with fire and brimstone** in the presence of the holy angels, and in the presence of the Lamb (Jesus): And the smoke of

> their torment ascendeth up for ever
> and ever: and they have **no rest
> day nor night...**"
>
> Revelation 14:10-11

God loves you so much that He gave you
many warnings about what hell is like. Please
don't believe the devil's lies any longer:

> "The Son of man (Jesus) shall send
> forth his angels, and they shall
> gather out of his kingdom all things
> that offend, and them which do
> iniquity; And shall cast them into
> a furnace of fire: there shall be
> **wailing and gnashing of teeth.**"
>
> Matthew 13:41-42

WHY WAS HELL CREATED?

At the beginning of the world, God made the
stars, planets, angels, people—everything!
One of the angels he created was named
Lucifer. Lucifer became proud, wanting to be
like God. So he rebelled against the Lord:

> "How art thou fallen from heaven, O
> Lucifer, son of the morning! how art
> thou cut down to the ground, which
> didst weaken the nations!
>
> For thou hast said in thine heart...
> I will be like the most High.
>
> Yet **thou shalt be brought down
> to hell,** to the sides of the pit."
>
> Isaiah 14:12-15

Lucifer persuaded one third of the angels to rebel with him. As punishment, God created the lake of fire, where He promised to send Satan and the fallen angels on Judgment Day.

Though the lake of fire was prepared for Satan and the angels who rebelled with him, those who obey and follow Satan will also be sentenced to the lake of fire:

> "The wicked shall be turned into hell, and all the nations that forget God."   Psalm 9:17

WHAT ABOUT YOU?

Now that you know what hell is **REALLY** like, does it sound like someplace you want to go?

Satan is going. His reservation is already in. It's just a matter of time before he hits the flames. Now, because he hates you, he wants to take you there as his "guest." Do you really want to join him?

Of course not! And luckily for all of us, God has made a way for us to escape the scorching fire of hell. Keep reading to discover the one and **ONLY** way you can escape this terrible place of torment.

The Secret About Sin

KURT COBAIN, the former lead singer for *Nirvana,* never learned this secret. As a result, he paid the ultimate price... death at age 27 and eternity in hell. Fortunately, you don't have to make the same mistake.

You see, sin played the same deadly trick on Kurt that it has played on hundreds of thousands of young people. Sin promised Kurt fame, power, money, thrills, sex, drugs, and anything else his heart wanted.

But sin never told him the horrible price he would have to pay, both while he was alive and after he died.

Sin promised Kurt great fun, but much of his life was a tormented existence. And when he might have been reaching out for help, sin pulled the plug and drove him to kill himself.

So many people have asked, "Why would such a talented young man end it all in the prime of life and at the peak of his career?"

A PEOPLE magazine article about his death tells about a grieving 20-year-old who kept a vigil outside Cobain's house since she heard he had killed himself. She said:

> "I came here looking for answers, **but I don't think there really are any.**"[1]

Yes, there *are* answers. But they're answers that sin is keeping well hidden from you.

The secret about sin is this: sin will promise you anything you want, but eventually, it will treat you the same way it treated Kurt Cobain. It will deceive you, torment you, and when it's done, *it will kill you!*

It's not hard to understand what happened to Kurt when you know how sin works. First sin entices you with promises of thrills and excitement. Then sin uses those thrills to wrap you up in bondage. Once you are under sin's control, it begins to torment you. And when sin has had it's fun, it kills you.

In his suicide note, Kurt showed how deceived

he had become, when he quoted some lyrics from a Neil Young song,

"It's better to burn out than fade away."

Kurt believed sin's lie that killing himself was the best solution. We'll talk more about suicide in the next chapter.

Of course, there were other factors in Kurt's death. Drugs and alcohol undoubtedly clouded his mind, and opened him up for control by demonic forces. But in the end, it was sin that had run it's course in Kurt's life.

It's tragic that a 27-year-old young man like Kurt Cobain had his life snuffed out because he never learned the truth about sin.

RIVER PHOENIX'S STORY

Sin deceived this famous young man too! It promised him stardom in both movies and television, plus riches and the worship of millions. No wonder sin's promises are so hard to resist.

Since those promises are sometimes granted for a short time, it's understandable that teens who are on the outside looking in want what these young "stars" have.

But sin never mentioned to River that late one night at the age of 23, his convulsing body would be lying on a garbage-lined Hollywood street, just moments from death.

And sin never mentioned to him that along

with the money and fame would come the incredible pressure to do drugs... drugs that would shortly take his life.

Although River Phoenix claimed he wasn't a drug abuser, when he died, his body contained toxic levels of cocaine and heroin, as well as traces of marijuana and valium.[2]

Neither River nor Kurt were bad people, they just never learned the truth about sin. As a result, sin deceived them, then it destroyed them.

MILLIONS MORE

Unfortunately, Kurt and River are not the only two young people who have been horribly deceived by sin. Despite their tragic deaths, millions of other teens are willingly throwing themselves into sin's deceptive traps:

> • Ted started smoking pot because he was sure it would make him cool and popular with the "in crowd," especially with the girls. Two years later, he was hopelessly hooked on cocaine. He spent every penny he could earn or steal to support his drug habit.

> • Candy's parents told her she shouldn't go out with Tony. But sin promised her she'd have a great time. She was convinced that she knew what she was doing. But

> today, rather than having fond
> memories of Tony, she remembers
> him as the man who gave her AIDS.

On and on the horror stories go. Every year, hundreds of thousands of teenagers learn the hard way that sin never gives them what it promises.

Though sin wraps itself in exciting looking packages, it's more deadly than a stick of dynamite. Sin may look beautiful from the outside, but it's a bomb that's ready to explode.

Each unfortunate teen who believes sin's lies is another victim of the master deceiver, Satan. And he is very convincing. By the time many young people learn they've been had—its too late. Their lives are shattered.

By the time a hungry fish realizes that the worm he was about to have for lunch was too good to be true, he's got a steel hook stuck through his mouth and is on his way to the frying pan. That's the same way Satan works.

You see, young person, the devil's only desire is to deceive and destroy you. So he pulls whatever sin he thinks will appeal to you out of his bag of tricks, wraps it in beautiful wrapping paper, sticks a bow on top of it, and lays it at your feet.

If you don't know the devil's secret about sin, you might not discover that it's a ticking time bomb until it blows up in your face.

THE TRUTH ABOUT SIN

God warned us about sin's consequences because He knew that Satan would tempt us with sin. And no matter what sin promises you, the consequence is death:

> "For the wages of sin *is death...*"
>   Romans 6:23

> "Then when lust hath conceived, it bringeth forth sin: and sin, when it is finished, *bringeth forth death.*"
> James 1:15

> "The soul that sinneth, *it shall die.*"
> Ezekiel 18:20

NOBODY GETS AWAY WITH SIN

Sadly, even many Christian teens today believe they can wallow in the filth of sin and get away with it. Satan whispers many lies in their ears, like:

- **"Nobody will ever know,"**
- **"You're not hurting anybody."**
- **"You're no worse than anyone else."**

Remember, Christian teen, when you play into Satan's hands, you are giving the enemy legal ground in your life. His ropes of bondage are tying you up, whether you know it or not.

And someday when you realize that you've been deceived and want out, you just may discover that you can't move.

That's because sin is like a heavy chain wrapping itself around you. The more you sin, the more often the chain encircles you and the heavier the weight becomes. Soon you are in total bondage—and you serve the sin whether you want to or not.

All sin brings people into bondage. When you serve sin, you become sin's servant:

> "Jesus said unto them... Whosoever committeth sin *is the servant of sin.*" John 8:34

No one gets away with sin, but because of the master deceiver's subtle devices, many, many people keep trying, thinking they'll be the first:

> "And the great dragon was cast out, that old serpent, called the Devil, and Satan, *which deceiveth the whole world...*" Revelation 12:9

> "And the devil *that deceived them* was cast into the lake of fire and brimstone..." Revelation 20:10

Be alert, young person. Satan is undoubtedly dangling a very tempting sin in front of you right now. It looks great, doesn't it? And I'm sure he is doing everything he can to convince you that no harm will come to you as a result of participating in it. *But he's lying!*

To make matters worse, the devil will use other people to entice you into his trap. He has many deceiving servants on the streets, who are looking for you:

> "But evil men and seducers shall wax worse and worse, *deceiving, and being deceived.*"
>
> 2 Timothy 3:13

> "That we henceforth be no more children, tossed to and fro, and carried about with every wind of doctrine, by the sleight of men, and cunning craftiness, whereby *they lie in wait to deceive.*"
>
> Ephesians 4:14

SIN: FREEDOM OR BONDAGE?

Satan's servants will assure you that sin will bring you excitement and thrills, but before you know it, you're in sin's bondage.

> "While they promise them liberty, they themselves are the servants of corruption: for of whom a man is overcome, *of the same is he brought into bondage.*"
>
> 2 Peter 2:19

Because God knows how sly the devil is, God specifically warns you:

> "Take heed to yourselves, that your heart *be not deceived...*"
>
> Deuteronomy 11:16

> "Little children, let no man *deceive*

you: he that doeth righteousness is righteous, even as he (Christ) is righteous. He that committeth sin is of the devil; for the devil sinneth from the beginning." 1 John 3:7-8

"Let no man deceive you with vain words: for because of these things cometh the wrath of God upon the children of disobedience."

Ephesians 5:1-6

WHAT IS SIN?

Sin is rebellion against God's commands. God wants to bless you, and since He knows that sin will block those blessings, He warned you to flee from it.

TACTIC #1

One of Satan's most successful tactics is to convince young people that:

"God just doesn't want you to have any fun!"

Nothing could be further from the truth. In reality, God doesn't want to see you suffer at the hands of the devil.

NIKKI'S STORY

Nikki was raised in a Christian home. She never drank, took drugs or did any of the other things that many of her classmates did. As she approached her teenage years, she wondered what sin was like. The kids at school made it sound fantastic.

So when Scott, the star of the football team,

asked her out, Nikki couldn't wait. Scott guaranteed her that she'd have the time of her life. She knew about Scott's wild reputation, but was willing to take the chance.

Satan convinced her that sin would give what it was promising, and take nothing in return.

After a wild night of partying, Scott started getting rough and began making sexual advances. Nikki got scared and tried to run. But Scott dragged her to his car, then drove to a deserted field where he raped her.

Nikki pressed charges, but three of Scott's football buddies lied for him and he walked free. The horrors of what happened that night will live in her memory for the rest of her life. Sin didn't give her what it promised. But then, it never does!

BROKEN PROMISES

No matter what the sin, it will never give you what it promises:

• **Alcohol** promises a great time as part of the "in crowd." But millions of alcoholics know that all alcohol delivers is a broken, shattered life and an early death.

• **Drugs** promise euphoric highs and an escape from reality. But they quickly bring you into bondage to Satan! Ask the multitudes who are hooked and trying to kick the habit how wonderful drugs are.

• **Satanism** promises you the desires of your heart. Power, money, sex, drugs. But those who have served Satan know that he may give a little for awhile, but when the dust settles, he *always* takes far more than he gives.

Sean began worshipping Satan, and dreaming of everything Satan would give him. Today he's rotting in a federal penitentiary—for murdering both of his parents in cold blood.

• **Rock music** promises thrills, excitement and freedom, but only brings bondage, suffering and early death. Don't believe it? Look how many rock stars are battling drug and alcohol addictions. Then check out how many moved to the cemetery at a young age.

In 1990, *Pearl Jam's* lead singer died of a heroin overdose,[3] as did Sid Vicious of the *Sex Pistols.* Drugs also took the life of rock guitar legend Alvin Lee. Drugs have taken the lives of so many rock musicians, it would take an entire book to list them all.

Yes, these people had fame for awhile. But Satan never told them the steep price they'd have to pay for that fame. He never does!

• **Rebellion** says, "It's your life... do what you want... don't let anyone tell you what to do!" Rebellion promises freedom—but millions of teens who believed that lie discovered the hard way that rebellion brings just the opposite—bondage and pain.

• **Immoral sex** promises pleasure beyond your wildest dreams, but that's not what it delivers. Instead, those who are deceived by this lie receive venereal diseases, unwanted pregnancies and AIDS.

Please don't be deceived, teen. Learn from all those who have gone before you. No one lives in sin and escapes its consequences. Sin is simply an enticing tool Satan uses to bring people into bondage to himself.

Your two choices are simple. Obey God and be set free, or obey Satan and live in bondage:

1. Obeying God may seem restrictive at first, but it's really protecting you from falling prey to Satan's destructive devices. Obeying God will set you free and allow you to enjoy happiness and contentment.

> "If the Son (Jesus) therefore shall make you free, ye shall be free indeed."   John 8:36

2. Obeying Satan and living in sin *always* leads to bondage.

I remember a teenager who learned this truth the hard way. He was once a heavy drug and alcohol user, with a hefty criminal record. But after being set free, he remarked:

> "I can't believe I was so deceived. Satan really had me fooled. I thought that sin would make me

free, but now I see that I was Satan's servant and he used sin to get me into bondage to him. But now, Jesus Christ has set me free from sin's grip and I have real peace in my heart."

The secret about sin is very simple. Sin always promises *freedom,* but the result is always *bondage.* From there, it's a cruel, downhill slide. Life becomes more miserable every day.

But the good news is that there is hope. That evil bondage can be broken, and you can be set free.

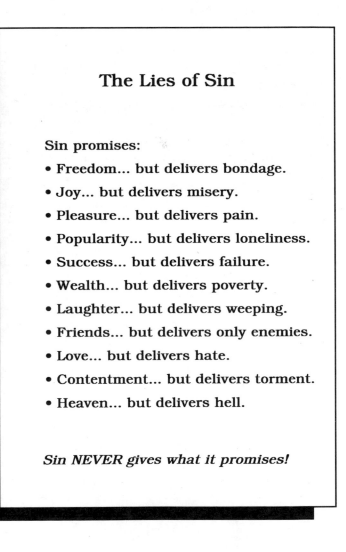

The Lies of Sin

Sin promises:

- Freedom... but delivers bondage.
- Joy... but delivers misery.
- Pleasure... but delivers pain.
- Popularity... but delivers loneliness.
- Success... but delivers failure.
- Wealth... but delivers poverty.
- Laughter... but delivers weeping.
- Friends... but delivers only enemies.
- Love... but delivers hate.
- Contentment... but delivers torment.
- Heaven... but delivers hell.

Sin NEVER gives what it promises!

The Secret About Suicide

TEENAGER... have you ever thought about ending it all?

Have you ever felt like life is so miserable that it's not worth living? If your answer is "yes," you definitely need to read on.

By the way, Christian teens are not immune from this epidemic. A recent study found that there was no difference in the percentage of Christian teens committing suicide and those who were not Christians.

Jerry Pounds, a seminary professor at New Orleans Baptist Theological Seminary, said:

"The fact is, there are just as many kids *in the church* committing suicide as outside the church."[1]

And the suicide statistics are staggering:

- Each year 6,500 teens commit suicide and another 400,000 try.[2]

That means more than 16 teens kill themselves *every day!*

- 1 out of every 3 teenagers has suicidal thoughts.
- 1 out of ever 6 teens attempts suicide sometime during their teenage years.
- 1 out of every 12 high school students attempted suicide last year.
- Every 38 seconds another teenager attempts suicide.

There are ten thousand reasons you might want to end your life. And only **YOU** know what's going on inside your head and why you might consider it.

A recent survey found that teens gave the following reasons for attempting suicide:[3]

- **Family Problems.............. 47%**
- **Depression 23%**
- **Problems with friends 22%**
- **Low self esteem 18%**
- **Boy/girl relationships 16%**
- **Feeling no one cares 13%**

Young person, your pain may be very real, even if you live in a Christian home. Many Christian parents have no idea how much inner pain their children are enduring.

These are difficult times for teens and it's understandable that you would consider extreme actions to end that pain.

Hundreds of teenagers have admitted to me that they were so depressed, they thought suicide was the *only* way to end their torment. No wonder the suicide rate among teens has doubled since 1968.[4]

AMBER'S STORY

Amber swallowed a whole bottle of pills to end her life. Why? It started when she was raped. She never told anybody about it and felt badly about herself.

> "I was feeling... like it was my fault— even though I know that that's really stupid. Then I started thinking that I was so ugly, and that nobody liked me. It's like a snowball kind of thing. I was feeling so down. It was like nothing was worth it at all."[5]

When she thinks about it now, Amber believes that her suicide attempt wasn't so much about wanting to end her life, but wanting to *"end her pain."*[6]

One report found that in three out of four cases, teens who had attempted suicide said that they felt "life wasn't worth living and had considered suicide as a way out."[7]

Brad wanted to end his pain, too! His father had sexually molested him since he was 4. As he grew up, he couldn't handle it, so he escaped into a world of heavy metal and drugs.

His grades dropped in school, his girlfriend dumped him and his parents got divorced. So Brad decided to leave home and live on his own.

With no money and no job, he got hungry enough to sell his body as a homosexual prostitute. Life was rapidly spiraling downward. Every move he made was the wrong one.

With no hope and a brain clouded by drugs, Brad figured suicide was the only way to end his pain. But he figured wrong...

THE SECRET

Listen closely, teen! Regardless of how painful your life is, and how much you are suffering, suicide is not the answer.

Suicide will **NOT** end your pain!

Because it is so important, here it is again.

Suicide will NOT end your pain!

In fact, unless your eternal destiny is settled, rather than ending your pain, suicide will launch you into an eternity of never-ending agony, far worse than anything you ever experienced on earth.

In chapter 2, you learned what hell is really like. It's heartbreaking to realize that young people are killing themselves, hoping for relief, but in reality, hell is all that awaits them.

THE CON-JOB

Teenager, if you don't learn anything else from this book, learn this: Satan and his demonic workers are the *only* ones who want you to kill yourself.

Here's the plan. First, the devil promises you a great time if you will partake of his sin. Then, once he sinks his evil hooks into you, he uses that sin to bring you into bondage.

Once he controls you, he makes your life so intolerable that you can't stand living. Then he whispers the thought in your mind, "Just kill yourself and end all this pain!"

What a con! Satan creates the original problem, then suggests a solution which is 100 times worse than the problem he created.

Tragically, millions of teens are falling for this con, and it's an eternal mistake that can never be undone. Can't you just hear Satan and his demons laughing at those who are victims of this eternally-damning trick.

If you want to end your pain, suicide is the *worst* choice you could make. If you think your problems are painful now, you haven't seen anything yet!

ADVERTISING

To deceive everyone he can, the devil is using every advertising vehicle at his disposal to make you believe that suicide is a good way to escape your pain.

Here's one of his most effective methods of getting this message to impressionable teens:

ROCK MUSIC

If you could step back from much of today's popular music for a second and take an objective look at it, you'd see that many of today's most popular music stars are being used (knowingly or unknowingly) by Satan.

For now, let's just consider suicide. Have you ever noticed how many people are singing songs suggesting that you kill yourself? Who really writes these songs... the singers... or Satan?

Superstar Michael Jackson gives us a clue:

> "I wake up from dreams and go, 'Wow! Put this down on paper!' The whole thing is strange. You hear the words, everything is right there in front of your face. And you say to yourself, *'I'm sorry, I just didn't write this.* It's there already.' I feel that somewhere, some place, it's

> all been done, and I'm the courier bringing it into the world."[8]

Michael is right. He is just a courier bringing Satan's message to millions of teens. You can't get too mad at Michael because he's just as deceived as those who listen to his music. (By the way, look at how the devil has treated Michael after all his years of faithful service.)

Former *Beatle* John Lennon says he received his songs the same way:

> "It's not a matter of craftsmanship; it (one of his songs) wrote itself. It drove me out of bed. I didn't want to write it... ***It's like being possessed; like a psychic or a medium.*** You have to get up, make it into something, and then you're allowed to sleep."[9]

Pearl Jam's lead singer, Eddie Vedder, confesses that his lyrics come the same way. He tells the story about how a friend of his gave him a cassette and told him that the guitarists on the tape were looking for a singer. Vedder listened to the tape, then went surfing.

The lyrics came to him, so he rushed back to his apartment, wrote three songs and recorded himself singing the lyrics over the melodies. He was in. And one of those songs became one of *Pearl Jam's* biggest hits, "Alive."[10]

It's no coincidence that another of *Pearl Jam's* biggest hits is a song called *Jeremy,* about a boy who kills himself in a classroom.[11]

When songs talk about death and killing, you can be sure that Satan wrote them, no matter whose name is on the CD.

Please understand, these musicians can't write lyrics with answers because they don't have any answers. Eddie Vedder admits where he's really coming from:

> "People think you are this grand person... because you are able to put your feelings into some song. They write letters and come to the shows... hoping we can fix everything for them. But we can't. What they don't understand is that you can't save somebody from drowning if you're treading water yourself."[12]

THEIR PURPOSE

You see, rock stars are preachers, preaching sermons Satan wants you to hear. Right now, he wants you to hear that suicide will end your pain. Listen to these popular rock lyrics:

> So you're looking for an anthem
> for a brand new age.
> It's not a fad, but it's a rage.
> This method is effective, tried and
> true.
> It's the only solution left for you.

Kill yourself, kill yourself
It's about time you tried
Kill yourself, kill yourself
It's about time you died.
Kill yourself — heed my advice
Kill yourself — take your life
Kill yourself — it's all for the best
Kill yourself — it's time for a rest.

Sadly, teenagers are listening to their rock idols... and are believing their false message that suicide will end their problems.

John, 19, shot himself to death with his father's .22 caliber pistol after listening to Osbourne's albums for several hours. He was still wearing headphones when his body was found.[13] Here are some lyrics to one of Ozzy's songs:

"Suicide Solution" Ozzy Osbourne

"Make your bed, rest your head
But you lie there and moan
Where to hide, *Suicide is the only way out*
Don't you know what it's all about?"

SUICIDE PACT

Nancy, 19, and Karen, 17, committed suicide together to end their problems. They shut themselves in an idling car.

A two-page suicide note written and signed by both girls contained lyrics to *Metallica's* "Fade To Black."[14]

"Fade To Black"

"Life it seems, will fade away
   Drifting further every day
Getting lost within myself
   Nothing matters.
I have lost the will to live
   Simply nothing more to give
There is nothing more for me
   Need to end to set me free."

Scott, 17, was found dead of carbon monoxide poisoning in his family's garage. In the suicide note he left to his girlfriend, Scott quoted the words from the same *Metallica* song.[15]

Please notice that the last line of that song is a bold faced lie. When you take your own life, you aren't "set free," you are doomed to an eternity of suffering in the lake of fire.

One fact you can always count on with Satan's preachers. They will lie to you *every* chance they get.

OTHER TOOLS

Rock music is not the only tool Satan is using to soften you up to the idea of suicide.

• Public schools now have classes on the subject, where teachers can suggest suicide as a possible problem solver.

• Many movies and T.V. shows have also explored the subject of suicide.

- Entire books have been published that teach you, step by step, how to kill yourself.

Yes, Satan is hard at work, ordering all his preachers to preach his favorite sermon from every pulpit he's got. The sermon is titled, "Suicide will end all your problems!"

DECISION TIME

Now that you know suicide will not end your pain, you must choose one of two roads...

- Believe the devil's lie and consider suicide as an option for ending your pain.

- Or keep reading and discover the only true way to solve your problems. You may think it's impossible, but that's because you've been listening to Satan for too long.

God has all power and is ready and willing to start working in your life, if you will let Him. And there is no question about what God is able to do:

> "With men this is impossible; but with God *all things are possible.*"
> Matthew 19:26

> "The things which are impossible with men *are possible with God.*"
> Luke 18:29

I'm not saying it will be easy, or that all your problems will disappear overnight, but I know that there is hope!

I've worked with hundreds of teenagers whose lives were so messed up that they tried to commit suicide. But as they learned the truth, their lives were transformed.

Yours can be too!

The Secret About Material Things

According to the world's standards, material things will bring you happiness. If that's the case, one of the happiest people who ever lived should have been former Beatle John Lennon.

He had millions of dollars, possessed worldwide fame, and enjoyed the worship of untold millions of people. Anything he could imagine owning, he could buy.

Was he happy?

We get a rare look inside the personal life of this former superstar through a letter he wrote to a preacher:

"Rev. Roberts,

This is ex-Beatle, John Lennon. I've been wanting to write to you, I guess I didn't want to face reality. I never do this, this is why I take drugs. Reality frightens me and paranoids me. True, I have a lot of money, being a Beatle, been all around the world, but basically I'm afraid to face the problems of life.

> **"As the song... Paul and me wrote, Money Can't Buy Me Love, it's true. The point is this, I want happiness... I want out of hell."**
>
> **Former Beatle John Lennon**

Let me begin to say, I regret that I said the Beatles were more popular than Jesus. I don't even like myself anymore, guilt. My Cousin, Marilyn McCabe has tried to help me. She told me you were praying for me.

Here's my life... Born in Liverpool, my mother died when I was little. My father left me at three. It was rough because just my aunt raised me. I never really liked her. I had an unhappy childhood, depressed a lot. Always missing my mom. Maybe if I'd had a father like you, I would have been a better person.

My own father I hate with a passion because he left my mom and me, came to me after we did *A Hard Day's Night* and asked for some money. It made me so mad, Paul had to hold me down. I was going to kill him. I was under the influence of pills at that time.

Married Cynthia, had a son John. I had to marry her, I really never loved her. She always embarrassed me walking around pregnant, not married, so I married her.

Only one regret, John has had to suffer a lot because recently she's been married again. He and me never get to see each other because Paul and I never got along anymore and that's how the four ended... As the song we wrote, Paul and me wrote, *Money Can't Buy Me Love*, it's true.

The point is this, I want happiness. I don't want to keep up with drugs. Paul told me once, 'you made fun of me for not taking drugs, but you will regret it in the end.'

Explain to me what Christianity can do

for me? Is it phoney? Can He love me? I want out of hell.

P.S. I am, I hate to say, under the influence of pills now. I can't stop. I only wish I could thank you for caring.[1]

John Lennon learned from experience that material things don't bring people happiness. They led him to the same destruction they've led many others to.

KURT COBAIN'S STORY

The same is true of former *Nirvana* lead singer, Kurt Cobain. He had a million dollar home, money, fame, power... all the trappings that many young people feel would bring them happiness. Yet he wanted to title *In Utero*, Nirvana's last album, *I Hate Myself and I Want To Die.*[2]

None of those material things brought him any happiness.

MICHAEL JACKSON'S STORY

How much happiness has Michael been able to buy with his multi-millions? Look what consumes his life. Allegations of child abuse. Treatment for drug addiction. Hounded day and night by the press. Family problems.

Michael is learning what many who have gone before him discovered... material things can't make an unhappy person happy.

O.J. SIMPSON'S STORY

Here's another man who had it all. A mansion in Brentwood, California, luxurious cars, fabulous vacations, and anything else he wanted.

And in one brief moment, his entire life was crushed. Whether he's guilty or innocent of the crimes he's charged with, one thing is certain—all the money in the world couldn't buy him happiness.

MICK JAGGER

Have millions of dollars and worldwide fame made Mick Jagger happy? Fellow *Rolling Stone* Keith Richards said this about Mick:

> "Ninety-nine percent of the male population of the Western world would give a limb to live the life of Jagger. *But he's not living a happy life.*"[3]

ANDY'S STORY

Andy isn't famous, but he learned the same secret. Andy lived a life that many teens only dream about living. He was young, single, and had lots of money. To make himself happy, he bought himself almost anything he desired.

The first toy Andy bought was an expensive sports car. But that didn't make him happy, so he traded it for a faster and more expensive one. That one didn't do the trick, either.

Next he bought an expensive house and filled it with lavish furniture, but still no happiness.

He treated himself to designer clothes and custom jewelry, but happiness still escaped him.

Andy tried the wild lifestyle, entertaining different women every night, drinking till early in the morning. Still no happiness.

He experimented with several types of drugs, but was still miserable.

When I met Andy, he was extremely depressed. He had accumulated all the material things he wanted, but none of them brought him the peace and contentment he was searching for. As we sat together one evening, Andy poured out his innermost feelings:

> "It feels like I've always had a great big hole in my heart. I've tried to fill it with everything I can think of but nothing works. I've tried drugs, alcohol, sex, material things, but nothing has filled that hole."

Then he asked me...

> "Do you know why those things won't fill that hole in my heart?"

It was then that I had the opportunity to explain to Andy why material things never bring happiness.

The Bible tells us that longing for money and what it can buy will bring you sorrows, not happiness:

> "For the love of money is the root of all evil: which while some coveted after, they have erred from the faith, **and pierced themselves through with many sorrows.**"
>
>   1 Timothy 6:10

Jesus Himself taught that there is much more to life than gathering up material things:

> "Take heed, and beware of covetousness (greed): for a man's life consisteth **not in the abundance of the things which he possesseth.**"
>
>   Luke 12:15

I went on to tell Andy the one and only way to fill that hole in his heart. In the next chapter, you'll learn what happened to Andy, but first, let's make sure that you understand that material things will never bring you real happiness.

BOMBARDED WITH LIES!

No wonder most young people think they can buy happiness. The media bombards youth with this false message at every turn.

• T.V. shows portray the rich and famous as having the ultimate in happiness. Yet, many of them live miserable lives, plagued by drugs, divorces, deceit and insecurity. No, being rich and famous does not guarantee happiness.

• Commercials try to convince you that their product will make you happy. But behind those promises is the harsh reality that they simply want your money.

• Movies, magazines and newspapers blast you with the message that money can buy happiness. But those who have lots of money have proven that it can't.

Don't be deceived. Collecting material things will never make you happy. Here are a few who've achieved what so many strive for. Let's see if it made them happy.

A MILLION DOLLAR WINNER

In 1987, 17-year-old James bought a Coke at a McDonald's in Norwalk, California. With it, he received a game ticket worth at least one million dollars. His first thought was:

> "I thought this would make me the happiest person I could be."[4]

But it didn't. Right from the start, problems arose. As an assistant manager at McDonald's, James was ineligible to receive the money. So he asked Teresa, a friend of his, to claim the winning ticket in return for half the profits.

But the two couldn't stop fighting. By 1990, Teresa had sued James, saying he had broken their contract.

In February, 1994, McDonalds learned about the agreement to split the winnings and sued the two to get their money back.

And even with $2,000 coming in every week, Teresa had financial problems. Her car was repossessed. Her boyfriend ran up big bills on her credit card, then disappeared. Her mother showed up needing money.

More legal battles followed. More lies, more deceit and more back-stabbing. In short, the money that was supposed to bring bliss to both these young people turned out to be the worst nightmare of their lives.

LOTTERY WINNERS

A TV show tracked down several people who had won multi-million dollar lotteries. Did they go on to live dream lives that you would drool over? Here are a few of their stories...

WIFE SHOT TO DEATH

When it was broadcast on the news that this couple had won several million dollars, the wife's ex-husband was so furious at the thought of his former wife and her new husband having all that money, he drove to her house and shot her to death.

When they interviewed the woman's present husband, he remarked that winning the lottery was the worst thing that had ever happened to him because it cost him his wife.

DESTROYED FAMILY

Another couple explained that when they won the lottery, everyone they knew expected to be given large amounts of cash. It created so much jealousy and bitterness among family members that the entire family was destroyed.

The wife said she wished they had never won because it cost her the people she loved.

FORCED INTO EXILE

Another couple who won the lottery was so hounded by an endless parade of people begging for money that their quiet, peaceful lifestyle was ruined. They were forced to sell their comfortable home and move to another state, where they now live in exile.

Several others reported that winning huge amounts of money brought them more misery than joy.

ONE MAN'S STORY

As far as the world knew, Jack Scalia had it made. By the time he was 29, he had been a professional baseball player and New York's highest paid male model. He had fame, money and all that goes with it.

Sounds great, doesn't it? Let's look behind the scenes and hear in Jack's own words what his life was really like.

"I started smoking marijuana and

> drinking when I was 12. Later on, I was taking 20 amphetamines a day. Soon cocaine and beer became the things I wanted most in life, although I took every other drug too, including LSD, heroin and speed."

Life got so bad, Jack even considered suicide:

> "I stood at my eighteenth-story hotel window. I was miserable and depressed: my fiancée had broken our engagement, I had alienated all my friends, my career had gone completely downhill. So I told myself, "Why not jump out this window? I have nothing to live for."

After having been there, let's here Jack's conclusion about material things:

> "I made a ton of money. I had a swanky penthouse apartment. I had a dream job. And I was the most miserable man on earth. I was a total loser."[5]

HOW TO FIND REAL HAPPINESS

Are you striving to accumulate material things, believing that they will bring you happiness? If so, you need to learn that happiness *never* comes from outside, it only comes from within. If you are happy on the inside, it won't matter how many material things you have.

Wouldn't you like to be really happy? Not the phony kind of happy you pretend to be in front of your friends, but a genuine peace and joy you feel deep down inside.

You can, but there's only *one* way to get it. That's what you'll learn in the next chapter...

6

The Most Important
Secret of All

When Andy asked if there was anything that would fill the hole in his heart, I explained that it could be filled, but not by any material thing. It would take a person to fill that hole... and only *one* person could do it... Jesus Christ.

> "That Christ may dwell *in your hearts* by faith..." Ephesians 3:17

> "To whom God would make known what is the riches of the glory of this mystery among the Gentiles; which is *Christ in you,* the hope of glory..."   Colossians 1:27

I explained to Andy that all people are sinners.

Adam and Eve, the first two people God created, opened the door to sin when they sinned in the Garden of Eden.

When they died, they passed that sin nature down to every person ever born. From then on, everyone who has lived inherited the sin nature from them.

> "For *all* have sinned, and come short of the glory of God;"
>
> Romans 3:23

Since God would never allow sin in heaven, He had to make a way for the sins of all mankind to be forgiven. That's why, almost 2,000 years ago, Jesus Christ (God the Son), left heaven and was born on earth as a little baby.

Jesus Christ loves you so much that He left the beauty of heaven to come here. While He walked the earth, people laughed at Him, mocked him and rejected Him:

- Some hated Him because He told them the truth.

- Religious leaders hated Him because He threatened their business.

- Sinners hated Him because He exposed their sin and made them feel very uncomfortable.

But because Jesus loves us so much, He took it all, and kept right on loving people.

Eventually, Jesus was brutally beaten and

nailed to a wooden cross. His executioners drove huge spikes into His wrists and feet, then hoisted the cross upright, where He suffered a torturous death.

But Jesus wasn't executed against His will. He went to the cross willingly. Jesus said:

> "No man taketh it (life) from me, but I lay it down of myself. I have power to lay it down, and I have power to take it again."   John 10:18

WHY DID HE DO ALL THIS?

Jesus suffered that awful death to pay the penalty for your sins, so you could escape hell and go to Heaven when you die.

> "For God so loved the world, that he gave his only begotten Son, that whosoever believeth in him should not perish, but have everlasting life."   John 3:16

That's real love... to literally die for someone else. The secret is that Jesus died in your place so your sins could be forgiven and you could receive the gift of eternal life. But you must accept Him as your personal Savior.

During the 33 years Jesus lived on earth, He never committed a single sin, or did anything wrong. He was able to do this because He was and still is God. The Bible says that people die as a result of sin:

> "For the *wages of sin* is death..."
>   Romans 6:23

Since Jesus never sinned, He wasn't required to die. So when He died, it wasn't for Himself, it was for us:

> "But God commendeth (proved) his love toward us, in that, while we were yet sinners, *Christ died for us.*"   Romans 5:8

Jesus' death made it possible for all of us to have our sins forgiven.

> "Without shedding of blood is no remission (forgiveness of sins)"
>   Hebrews 9:22

A FREE GIFT

Young person, God Almighty wants to give you a free present, eternal life in heaven with Him.

> "*...the gift of God* is eternal life through Jesus Christ our Lord."
> Romans 6:23

Many people think they must do good works to reach heaven. But God's Word says that we are saved by faith in Jesus Christ, not by good works:

> "For by grace are ye saved through faith; and that not of yourselves: it is the gift of God: *not of works,*

lest any man should boast."

Ephesians 2:8-9

To receive this gift of eternal life, you must do two things:

1. **Repent:** The Bible tells us that if we will not repent (turn away from our sinful old lifestyles), there is no hope for us.

   "...except ye repent, ye shall all likewise perish."   Luke 13:5

2. **Trust Jesus Christ** alone for your salvation:

   "That if thou shalt confess with thy mouth the Lord Jesus, and shalt believe in thine heart that God hath raised him from the dead, thou shalt be saved. For with the heart man believeth unto righteousness; and with the mouth confession is made unto salvation."

   Romans 10:9-10

That's the **ONLY** way to get your sins forgiven:

"...the blood of Jesus Christ cleanseth us from all sin."   1 John 1:7

And that's the *only* way to fill that big empty hole in your heart. That's exactly what Andy did that night. After years of searching for happiness, he bowed his head and cried out to Jesus, praying a prayer like this:

Dear Lord Jesus:

My life is a wreck. I've tried everything I can think of to fill the hole in my heart, but nothing has worked. Please come into my heart and fill it.

I admit that I'm a sinner and I deserve to go to hell, but right now I accept You as my Savior. I ask you to come into my life and change me into what you want me to be. Thank you for saving me. Amen.

As tears poured down Andy's face, it was obvious that he'd finally found what he had spent so many years searching for. His face glowed as he began to experience the joy of knowing Jesus Christ.

I heard from Andy a few weeks later. His message went something like this:

Finally, that hole in my heart is filled, and I feel a perfect peace inside. Now I don't need any of the things I used to want so much. Jesus is what I was searching for all along.

At last I have peace and joy in my life. I know why I'm here on earth and where I'm going when I die. I never thought I could feel this good.

This is what everyone needs... to have Jesus living in their heart.

WHAT ABOUT YOU?

The Bible gives you this same promise. If you will admit that you are a sinner and will invite Jesus Christ into your heart, you can be saved right now:

> "For whosoever shall call upon the name of the Lord *shall be saved.*"   Romans 10:13

Jesus wants to forgive you, no matter how cold you feel or how far you've strayed. The man who wrote more books of the Bible than anyone else was a murderer. God called King David "a man after mine own heart" even though he committed adultery and murder.

That's because God forgave him when he repented of his sins. God wants to do the same for you.

If you would like to accept Jesus Christ as your Lord and Savior, pray a sincere prayer from your heart like this:

> Dear Lord Jesus,
>
> I'm a sinner. I know I deserve to go to hell, but I believe that You died on the cross to take my place and pay the price for my sins. I accept You as my personal Savior. I ask you to come into my heart. Please

> forgive all my sins and save me
> right now. Thank you, Lord Jesus.
> Amen.

Teen, if you just prayed a prayer like that and meant it with all your heart, then God's Word promises two things just happened to you:

1. You just became a child of God:

> "But as many as received him
> (which you hopefully just did), to
> them gave he power to become *the
> sons of God,* even to them that
> believe on his name:"   John 1:12

2. You will go to heaven when you die and will live with God forever:

> "He that heareth my word, and
> believeth on him that sent me, *hath*
> everlasting life, and shall not come
> into condemnation; but is passed
> from death unto life."   John 5:24

There is no other way to get to heaven or to fill that empty space in your heart. Jesus Christ is the *only* way.

> "Neither is there salvation in *any*
> other: for there is *none* other name
> under heaven given among men,
> whereby we must be saved."
>   Acts 4:12

If you haven't already accepted Christ, please don't let the devil keep you in his evil grasp any longer. Turn your back on all the deadly lies he's dangling in front of you.

HUNDREDS OF OTHERS

Jesus has been the answer for *every* young person I've ever worked with, no matter what their problem. He's healed drug addicts, prostitutes, thieves, runaways, you name it. No problem is too big for Him.

These young people had been deceived by Satan and were headed for ruin. But when they accepted Christ's gift of eternal life, Satan lost another slave, and God adopted another child into His family.

Right now, *you* can experience that same joy.

PLEASE DON'T PUT IT OFF

Teen, you need Jesus Christ in your life. And the time to receive Him is right now:

> "Behold, *now* is the accepted time;
> behold, *now* is the day of salvation."
> 2 Corinthians 6:2

Jesus loves you and is patiently waiting for you. Remember, there's no guarantee that you will be around tomorrow. Trust Christ now, before it is forever too late!

7

Who's Your Best Friend?

KRISTIN AND MIKE WERE IN LOVE. Mike promised Kristin that there would never be anyone else in his life, and that he wanted to spend the rest of his life with her. They talked about marriage and even a family.

With promises like those, Kristin felt comfortable becoming sexually active with Mike.

After a few months, Kristin learned that she was pregnant. She couldn't wait to share the good news with Mike, thinking he'd be thrilled.

He wasn't!

In fact, Mike pressured Kristin for several

weeks to have an abortion. The truth was that he didn't want to be financially responsible for this child.

When Kristin, in tears, told Mike that she could never murder her baby, he disappeared and never returned.

Eight months later, Kristin lay alone in a delivery room, giving birth to a beautiful baby girl. As she hugged her child for the first time, she realized that she alone would be responsible for providing for this infant.

Kristin couldn't believe that Mike had deserted her. He was her best friend. She thought she could count on him. He was the one person she thought would never leave her.

Unfortunately, it's not uncommon for teens to be deserted by their closest friends, especially when they need them the most. You may know how Kristin felt because a friend may have deserted you in a time of crisis.

YOUR WISH CAN COME TRUE

Have you ever wanted a friend who would never turn on you, especially when you are in big trouble? If so, that wish can come true.

If you just received Jesus into your heart, you now have such a friend. Jesus is the best friend you could ever have.

> "And the Lord, he it is that doth go before thee; he will be with thee,

> *he will not fail thee, neither*
> *forsake thee:* fear not, neither be
> dismayed." Deuteronomy 31:8

Satan makes sure that his evil world system
always portrays Jesus in the worst possible
light. The world seldom uses the name of
Jesus as anything more than a curse word.
But don't be deceived. You could never have a
better friend than Jesus Christ.

As you just learned, because Jesus loves you,
He died a painful death on the cross so you
could have God's gift of eternal life.

ANOTHER BENEFIT

But going to heaven isn't the only benefit to
getting saved. Jesus wants to be your best
friend and meet your every need right now.

Yes, teen, Jesus really does love you and
care about you. He knows everything you are
feeling right now. When your heart aches, His
does too!

And God's love for you isn't based on how well
you perform. He loves you because of who you
are, not because of what you do. Many people
only love those who perform in an acceptable
manner, but Jesus loves you just the way you
are. And His love will **NEVER** change:

> "Jesus Christ the same yesterday,
> and to day, and for ever."
> Hebrews 13:8

How many friends do you have that would lay down their life for you? You have one, because Jesus already did. That is the greatest act of love that there is:

> "Greater love hath no man than this, that a man lay down his life for his friends."   John 15:13

And that's just the beginning of what Jesus wants to do for you. There's plenty more:

1. Jesus wants to guide you through life, helping you avoid the deadly traps Satan has laid for you.

> "Trust in the Lord with all thine heart; and lean not unto thine own understanding. In all thy ways acknowledge him, and *he shall direct thy paths."* Proverbs 3:5-6

> "The steps of a good man are ordered *by the Lord:* and he delighteth in his way."   Psalm 37:23

Many teens are confused about the future. Kurt Cobain made a fortune proclaiming how hopeless life was and how dismal the future looked. Young people flocked to him because they identified with what he was saying.

But with Jesus in your life, God will guide every step you take. And even if something happens that you think is bad, God will use it for your good:

"And we know that *all* things work together for good to them that love God, to them who are the called according to his purpose."

Romans 8:28

2. Jesus wants to protect you.

"For he (God) shall give his angels charge over thee, to keep thee in all thy ways. They shall bear thee up in their hands, lest thou dash thy foot against a stone."

Psalm 91:11-12

"The angel of the Lord encampeth round about them that fear him, and delivereth them."   Psalm 34:7

Can you imagine how great it would be to have divine protection? Especially today, with rapes, murders, kidnappings, etc. Well, God can and will post his angels around you to protect you—if you'll give your life to Him.

3. Jesus wants to meet all your needs:

"But my God shall supply *all your need* according to his riches in glory by Christ Jesus."

Philippians 4:19

"O fear the Lord, ye his saints: for *there is no want* to them that fear him."   Psalm 34:9

God loves taking care of His children. He wants

to meet *all* your needs—physical, emotional, spiritual—*all* of them.

> "The Lord is my shepherd; *I shall not want."*   Psalm 23:1

> "I have been young, and now am old; yet have I not seen the righteous forsaken, nor his seed begging bread."   Psalm 37:25

4. Jesus wants to take away all your fears:

> "The Lord is my helper, and *I will not fear what man shall do unto me."*   Hebrews 13:6

Everyone experiences fear to some degree. Fear of certain people, fear of the future, fear of failure, fear of the unknown...

How exciting it is to realize that God wants to take all your fear and replace it with peace and confidence in Him. You don't have to live in fear any longer.

> *"For God hath not given us the spirit of fear;* but of power, and of love, and of a sound mind."
>   2 Timothy 1:7

> "There is *no fear* in love; but perfect love casteth out fear: because fear hath torment."
>   1 John 4:18

Judy thought satanism would be fun. But

once she got on the inside, she saw things she wished she had never seen.

When she wanted out, they threatened to kill her entire family. For several months she was terrified—convinced that there was no way out.

Then Judy learned that God has a hundred million times more power than Satan, and if she became God's child, all that fear could be taken away.

When a Christian speaks in the name and authority of Jesus Christ, all evil beings must cower in obedience. Satan can do **NOTHING** to God's children unless God allows it.

5. Jesus wants to place peace in your heart. Jesus said:

> "Peace I leave with you, my peace I give unto you: not as the world giveth, give I unto you. Let not your heart be troubled, neither let it be afraid."   John 14:27

Though the whole world is in turmoil, Jesus can give you peace:

> "Thou (God) wilt keep him *in perfect peace,* whose mind is stayed on thee."   Isaiah 26:3

> "And the peace of God, which passeth all understanding, shall keep your hearts and minds through Christ Jesus."   Philippians 4:7

Unsaved teens don't have a chance because their master *never* gives his children peace.

And sad to say, far too many Christian teens seldom experience God's peace either. Usually it's because they are lusting after the things of the world. The lust of the flesh, the lust of the eyes and the pride of life are very appealing, but they *always* steal your peace.

But if you dedicate yourself to finding and doing God's will for your life, you will experience a peace the world knows nothing about.

That's not to say you won't have any problems, but there is a wonderful peace in knowing that the Lord is directing your life.

6. Jesus wants to give you joy:

> "Thou wilt shew me the path of life: in thy presence is *fulness of joy:* at thy right hand there are pleasures for evermore."   Psalm 16:11

Jesus would love to fill your heart with joy, just as he's done for hundreds of thousands of other teens.

> "These things have I spoken unto you, that my joy might remain in you, and *that your joy might be full.*   John 15:11

You don't have to let the devil steal the joy God wants you to have.

WHAT A FRIEND!

These are just a few of the wonderful things your best friend is longing to do for you. There are many more. And the best part is, He will NEVER forsake you, especially during the hard times when you need Him the most.

But for Jesus to be YOUR best friend, you must first be born into God's family. If you haven't done that yet, please go back and read the last chapter again.

If you are already a Christian, why not pray a prayer like this, and mean it:

> Dear Lord Jesus,
>
> I confess every sin that I have committed, and I ask you to forgive me for each one. Please wash me with your blood and restore my fellowship with you.
>
> Please help me to turn my back on the lustful things of the world so I can hear your voice as you lead me.
>
> Please fill me with peace and joy, and live your life through me.
>
> Thank you, Lord, for being my best friend. In Jesus' name, Amen.

8

How To Be Really Happy

EXCITEMENT WAS IN THE AIR. It was the day the whole town had been waiting for. The annual slave auction was about to begin.

It was a crisp, clear morning along the banks of the Mississippi River. A long line of slaves stood chained to each other ready to be sold. But one particular slave made this year's auction an event not to be missed.

His name was Joe. He was 6'6" tall and 275 pounds of pure muscle. Every slave owner in the state dreamed of owning Joe because of his superior strength and abilities.

One by one, the slaves were sold to the highest

bidder. Soon it was time for Joe to be led to the block where everyone could view him.

Everyone knew that the richest and meanest man in the state was at the auction for one purpose... to buy Joe and work him to death.

Meanwhile, a wealthy merchant was sailing by at the time. He noticed the gathered crowd and asked what was taking place. The merchant instructed that his ship be taken to shore.

He hiked up a steep hill and stood at the back of the crowd as Joe was stepping up on the block. The merchant chatted with a stranger next to him and learned about Joe and the farmer who was planning to buy him.

The bidding began. Back and forth it went until there were only three bidders left. Then the rich farmer shouted out, "I double my last bid." A stunned silence fell over the crowd. It was over! Certainly nobody could top that bid. Joe was doomed to a life of suffering!

The auctioneer raised his gavel and hollered:

> "Going once, going twice, going... going... "

Then, from the back, the merchant yelled out:

> **"I double the last bid."**

The audience gasped! The farmer, in a rage, turned and stalked away, for he could not afford to top that bid.

The merchant approached the front and paid for his new property. But instead of taking his slave away, he unlocked the shackles, looked Joe in the eyes and said, "you're free to go."

Joe stared in disbelief as this stranger explained:

> "I don't believe in owning slaves. I just couldn't stand the thought of a cruel taskmaster owning you. The only reason I paid the price was to set you free."

Joe replied,

> "No one has ever shown that kind of love for me. I have nowhere else to go and there is no way I could survive on my own. Could I please come with you and serve you in thanks for what you've done for me?"

So Joe faithfully served his new-found friend for the rest of his life, fully content knowing that he was serving a man who loved him and had given him his life back.

EVERYBODY SERVES SOMEBODY

Whether you realize it or not, teen, everybody serves somebody. You are serving someone right now. Either you are serving God or you are serving the devil.

If you are thinking to yourself: "I don't serve anybody. I do what *I* want," then you are serving the devil... you just don't know it. You can tell who you serve by who you obey:

> "Know ye not, that to whom ye yield yourselves servants to obey, *his servants ye are to whom ye obey;* whether of sin unto death, or of obedience unto righteousness?"
>
> Romans 6:16

When you serve your own flesh, you are serving the devil. When you deny yourself and obey God's will, then you are serving God.

THE SECRET

The world will tell you that if you serve yourself and do what you want, you 'll be happy.

At the same time, you are led to believe that if you submit your life to God and serve Him, your life will be miserable. In fact, the exact opposite is true.

If you serve your flesh (Satan), you may have some fun for awhile, but you will suffer in the end.

But if you willingly submit yourself to God, real happiness can be yours. True peace and contentment only occur when God has control of your life and you live in submission to His will.

The story at the beginning of this chapter perfectly illustrates your life. Satan is a cruel taskmaster who wants to grind you to powder.

But when Jesus died on the cross, He bought you with His blood. If you will receive Him as your Savior, He will unlock the shackles that Satan has on you, *and He'll set you free!*

When Joe was set free, it wasn't a burden for him to work for the merchant. He was glad to serve the one who had given him everything.

In the same way, when a person is set free from Satan's grasp by the power of Jesus Christ, it isn't a drudgery to serve Him, it's a pleasure.

If you think you will ever find happiness while wearing a ball and chain under a ruthless master like Satan, you are making a huge mistake. Happiness only comes when Jesus Christ cuts the shackles off.

ED'S STORY

Ed was a typical teenager. He wanted to be part of the "in" crowd, and was willing to do whatever it took to get there. So he drank, took drugs and did whatever his "friends" wanted him to.

Eventually, Ed realized that all these flesh-pleasing activities were not bringing him popularity, but they were leading him into deeper and deeper bondage to Satan.

After several months, Ed finally admitted that his life was a mess and he felt like dying. The worst part was that he didn't have a clue how to turn his life around.

WHAT WOULD MY FRIENDS THINK?

One day a friend invited Ed to church. Ed snickered to himself:

> "I've been to church all my life, and all I've ever seen is hypocrisy. Besides I'm too cool to be seen going to church. What would my friends think?"

But his friend persisted, so Ed agreed to go. While the pastor was preaching, the Holy Spirit of God was speaking to his heart and drawing him to salvation. At the end of the sermon, Ed felt so drawn that he stepped out and made his way to the front.

That day, Ed trusted Jesus Christ as his personal Savior. He gave up control of his life and turned it over to Jesus. He thought:

> "This is weird. I never thought that I could willingly submit myself to anyone's authority. I was sure that I'd hate it, but here I am giving total control of my life to Jesus Christ, and I feel *great* about it."

Ed was learning that God can run our lives far better than we could ever hope to, and that true happiness only comes when He is guiding our lives.

In the months that followed, Ed learned a secret that many teens (and adults) have never learned. Submitting to God and fulfilling His will is the *only* way to find lasting peace and happiness.

YOU CAN BE HAPPY TOO!

If you want to be happy, there's only *one* way. Stop trying to please yourself and give control of your life to God.

> "...whoso trusteth in the Lord, *happy* is he."   Proverbs 16:20

> "*Happy* is he that hath the God of Jacob for his help, whose hope is in the Lord his God:"   Psalm 146:5

WHERE DID IT START?

This "satisfy yourself and you'll be happy" lie started shortly after man was created. When God made Adam and Eve, He told them not to eat of a certain tree. Had they obeyed, they could have enjoyed perfect peace in the presence of God forever.

But along came Satan with a lie that he's still using today. He enticed Eve with big promises. All she had to do was reject God's Word and eat this delicious looking piece of fruit.

So Eve ate, then convinced Adam to eat. As a result of their disobedience, they were both kicked out of the Garden of Eden. They learned that, despite what Satan tells you, disobeying God **NEVER** brings happiness, just pain, misery and suffering.

DANA'S STORY

Dana was born and raised in a strict Christian home. Her parents loved her and wanted the best for her. To protect her, they instituted a long list of rules and regulations.

They watched every step she took, fearful that Satan would get a foothold in their daughter's life.

They didn't know it, but Dana began feeling suffocated. She started thinking, "I want to do what *I* want." In reality, she wanted to partake of the sins Satan was dangling in front of her. She wanted to please her flesh. And the devil made those sins look very appealing.

Little by little, Dana's actions followed the desires of her heart. But something unexpected happened. The joy and satisfaction she expected never came. Instead, a heaviness she had never felt overcame her.

Dana recognized what was happening and learned that happiness is never gained by listening to Satan and obeying his desires. Happiness comes only when you obey God's will for your life.

So late one night, Dana knelt by her bed and poured her heart out to God. Her prayer went something like this:

> Heavenly Father, I know that I fell for Satan's lies. I rebelled against

my parents, thinking I could find happiness doing what I wanted. I now realize that I was really rebelling against You and that You are the *only* One who can give me real happiness. I'm sorry.

Lord, please restore my relationship with You. I thank You for loving me even when I fail. In Jesus' name, Amen.

When Dana finished praying, the heaviness in her heart was gone. Her burdens were lifted. Joy and peace were restored. She sat up on her bed and laughed for several minutes. She knew that the bondage of sin had been broken off and she worshipped God for the rest of the night.

From then on, obeying Christ's requests was no longer a burden. Instead, Dana looked at each one as the desire of her Heavenly Father. She was happy to comply. And the more she obeyed, the more peace and joy she felt.

Like Joe, Dana made up her mind that night to willingly serve God in thanks for what He had done for her.

If you are not experiencing peace like Dana, maybe it's because you are serving the wrong master. If you are a Christian, but feel no peace or happiness inside, maybe it's because you are serving the wrong master.

Which do you long to do?

- **Feed the lusts of your flesh.**
- **Joyfully serve the One who set you free.**

Be honest. If you long to feed the lusts of your flesh, you are serving Satan, and he will *never* make you happy. Satan "blesses" his servants with gifts like drug addiction, loneliness, alcoholism, fear, AIDS, venereal diseases, death... but never happiness.

On the other hand, if you are overcome with gratefulness to God for setting you free, and you only want to please Him in everything you do, you can be sure that happiness will follow.

KELSEY'S STORY

Kelsey was a Christian teen who believed that happiness came by having lots of friends. She was sure that if she became a cheerleader, she would reach that goal.

But the more friends she accumulated, the more problems she encountered.

Life turned so sour that Kelsey eventually wondered if life was even worth living. It was then that she looked up towards heaven and realized that she had been deceived.

She cried out to God and asked Him to forgive her. She promised to give Him total control of her life.

Within days, all the burdens were gone... trying to be cool... trying to please others... talking and acting the right way... she didn't care about any of that anymore.

As Kelsey grew spiritually, her goal was to deny herself and do what God led her to do. The more she pleased God, the happier she felt.

YOU CAN BE HAPPY TOO!

There is hope! You can be happy, if you will give the Lord total control of your life. No matter how much turmoil you are facing, God's promises are true.

> "...*happy* is that people, whose God is the Lord.   Psalm 144:15

IT'S DECISION TIME

If you are a Christian, the first question you must answer is, "Who am I going to serve? The Lord Jesus Christ, or my flesh? (Satan)

If you decide to please your flesh, you'll never be happy. But if you dedicate yourself to pleasing Christ, your loving Heavenly Father will fill you with peace and joy that nobody can take away.

In the next chapter, you're going to learn why somebody may be hoping that your life falls apart.

9

You're Worth a Fortune... On One Condition

JAMES DIED on the emergency room table. If only he had learned this secret, his life could have been saved.

The end came on a Friday night. James was taking his girlfriend to see their favorite rock group in concert. He had gladly shelled out $100.00 for two tickets. But that was only a fraction of his total investment.

James had bought all five of the groups C.D.'s at $15.00 apiece. He also owned three of the band's T-shirts—$12.00 each. His bedroom was cluttered with several rock magazines containing articles and photos of the group.

And several expensive color posters of his heroes hung on his bedroom walls.

On his way to pick up his girlfriend, James stopped by his dealer's house and purchased enough drugs for the evening—then detoured to a convenience store and laid out some more cash for two six packs of beer and three packs of cigarettes.

IT WASN'T SUPPOSED TO END LIKE THIS!

They arrived at the arena early, and after paying $5.00 to park the car, the two eagerly got the party started.

After about an hour, James passed out. His girlfriend, in a panic, got some help and rushed him to a hospital emergency room.

The receptionist collected James' insurance card, then had him raced to an examination room. They worked furiously on him for an hour, but lost the battle. James died.

James' parents and his close friends grieved this young man's death. But they were not alone. Another group was also saddened, but for a different reason. This group grieved because they couldn't make any more money off James.

You see, James had helped fund the lavish lifestyle of many people, but they all had one thing in common. For them to be successful, James had to be wrecking his life.

THE SECRET

If you are in any kind of trouble, you can bet that there are people out there who hope you will stay that way. In fact, their livelihood depends upon it.

If you're not in trouble yet, somebody right around the corner probably has his eye on you, and is devising a way to make some money at your expense.

This is one of the saddest secrets of all. You are worth a lot of money to someone... under one condition... you will have to *suffer*... and maybe even *die*... for them to profit.

Many people are so deceived by Satan that they view you as nothing more than a business opportunity, a commodity they can use to make themselves rich. The enemy blinds them to the fact that your life may be torn to shreds in the process. Here are a few examples:

DRUGS

There's no question that drugs are killing teens, both Christian and non-Christian. There is also no question that those who sell drugs are making enormous amounts of cash.

- Cocaine creates 26 to 32 **billion** dollars a year in income.[1]

- The illegal drug industry is America's second largest business. Only Exxon is larger.[2]

• The drug paraphernalia business is a
  multi-billion dollar annual industry.[3]

If you are among the millions of teens who take
drugs, you are helping to make people rich—
people who are feeding you a poison that will
eventually destroy your life.

Have you ever thought that if you quit drugs,
the person you buy from and everyone up the
line from him or her would lose money.

TWO BROTHERS

When John died of a drug overdose, his dealers
had to find another customer to keep the cash
flowing in. They did—John's kid brother, Joe.

They led Joe down the same road. He had
an expensive drug habit, and his brain was
almost gone. He wandered aimlessly, a total
vegetable.

I watched Joe's father, a medical doctor,
slump down in a chair and weep over losing
another son to drugs. But for Joe's suppliers it
was just a business setback.

THE NETWORK

The whole drug network runs the same way.
While street dealers use those who take the
drugs, the dealers are being used by those
above them.

On it goes, all the way to the big shots, who
live in guarded mansions, with layers of people

between them and their drugs. Everyone uses those below them.

And those at the very top, who think they are running the show, are really being used by Satan. And when the devil is finished with them, he'll destroy them too.

DRUG EDUCATION IN PUBLIC SCHOOLS

Many public schools now employ what is called "nondirective education." Rather than telling you in school that drugs are wrong, they teach you about drugs, then tell you to make your own decisions. *The Phyllis Schlafly Report* reveals who's supporting this:

> "It's no accident that the R.J. Reynolds Tobacco Company is a contributor to this type of nondirective drug education course. They are using the public schools as part of a marketing plan to tell the little fourth graders and fifth graders that they have the capacity to make this decision and don't need to listen to any other authority."[4]

And the tobacco companies are doing their job well. In a recent survey, 91% of all 6-year-olds knew who Joe Camel was. Mickey Mouse barely beat him out at 96%.[5]

The tobacco companies don't care that in just one year there were 419,000 tobacco related deaths.[6] That's over 49 people dying *every single hour,* every day of the year.

What matters to them is recruiting new smokers to keep the dollars flowing in. Rep. Richard Durbin of Illinois says:

> "If we can reduce the number of young smokers, the tobacco companies will be in trouble *and they know it.*"[7]

WHAT'S AT STAKE?

The tobacco industry produces **$48 BILLION** dollars a year.[8] With that kind of money at stake, they'll gladly start warping the minds of fourth and fifth graders, so they can convert them into a customer as early as possible.

> In 1993, $339.8 million was spent on cigarette ads.[9]

As a result of those ads, about 1 million new teens start smoking each year. That's 3,000 teens a day, even though most are too young to buy cigarettes legally.[10] And once they are hooked, not many overcome their addiction and quit.

Now the government has learned that a tobacco company which produces several popular brands of cigarettes has been growing tobacco that is genetically engineered to have twice the normal nicotine and has been using the leaves in its cigarettes.[11]

With twice the nicotine, the cigarettes are

twice as addictive—and twice as hard to quit. They're also twice as profitable.

WHY TEENS SMOKE

Studies show that teens start smoking for two main reasons—rebellion and peer pressure. Cigarette advertisers appeal to both desires to make you think you are really cool when you smoke. But you're not. Shrewd businessmen are using you to line their pockets with cash.

One sophomore recalls her first smoke:

> "I remember sitting there and thinking—I was cool, I'm a rebel. Now, I look back, and I was such a dork."[12]

When you smoke, you may look like you're being cool, but you're really just blackening your lungs and killing yourself. And there's nothing cool about paying someone to kill you.

SEX EDUCATION

While we're talking about public schools, guess who's pushing sex education classes in school:

> "It's no accident that a leading contraceptive manufacturer is a leading promoter of sex education in schools. They want to create a new market among young people for their products."[13]

The makers of contraceptives don't care about your health or well-being. They want you to keep having sex so you'll need their product. If their product fails and you contract a venereal disease or AIDS, that's your problem, not theirs.

ROCK MUSIC

I remember driving past Rod Stewart's sprawling Beverly Hills mansion and thinking about the horrible price that thousands of young people have paid to buy him that home.

When Lisa paid $50 to hear Rod sing "Tonight's The Night" in concert, she wasn't thinking about the night a few months later when she would lay terrified on a table in an abortion clinic, about to end her unborn baby's life.

Then I pictured Rod, lounging by his pool, soaking up some sun, safe and secure behind his iron gates. He doesn't lose any sleep over the fact that his luxurious lifestyle came at the expense of teens like Lisa. No, her destruction was his ticket to wealth.

The rock stars must have a good laugh over the fact that teens fall for their scam. They rake in millions through concerts, tapes and CD's, preaching to impressionable young people that happiness comes from immorality, rebellion, drugs, alcohol and suicide.

They even use these themes to mass market T-shirts, videos, posters, magazines, jewelry, and anything else that will earn a buck.

Then, while teens are out destroying themselves, the rock stars retreat to their lavish mansions and count their money, reaping the financial benefits of ruined teenage lives.

What's just as sad, though, is that the rock stars, who are deceiving teens, are also being deceived by Satan. The devil may give them a few carrots to gnaw on for a while, but when they least expect it, their lives will be snatched from them, and they will be sent to hell.

ALCOHOL

- Three drunk teenagers hit a concrete wall at 80 MPH and died instantly.

- Tanya always got depressed when she drank. One night she got so depressed she hung herself.

- Julie hated to see her father drink because he sexually molested her every time he did.

These are just three of the many ways that alcohol is killing teens while it lines the pockets of those who produce it.

A magazine ran an article entitled "Liquor Profits Runneth Over." The article reported that in one year, the four leading alcohol producers sold $17 billion worth of alcohol."[14]

The article said that only one other packaged goods business regularly produces numbers like that—*the tobacco industry.*"[15]

How's their outlook for the future? Says one executive from a major liquor company:

> "We've never made more money in our history, and our forecasts are for very dynamic growth from distilled spirits for years to come."[16]

IT DOESN'T GET ANY BETTER THAN THIS?

Who's drinking all this liquor? And what kind of price are they paying to keep these alcohol producers rolling in the dough?

Michael Shingledecker and a friend of his decided to copy a stunt they had recently seen in the movie *The Program.* So they both laid down in the road between the yellow stripes on busy Route 62 in central Pennsylvania.

Michael was run over and killed instantly. Experts said that both he and his friend had consumed enough beer to "impair their mental functions."[17]

Alcohol is impairing the mental functions of scores of teens. The results are devastating:

> "Alcohol-related accidents are the leading cause of death among teen-agers."[18]

> "40% of all teenage deaths result from auto crashes, of which half are alcohol-related."[19]

> "25,000 Americans were killed in

1988 in auto accidents involving alcohol."[20]

Former Secretary of Health and Human Services Otis Bowen stated that alcohol is involved in *one out of every three cases of child molestation.*"[21]

And 3 of every 10 adolescents have drinking problems—*nearly 5,000,000* young people.[22]

A Gallup Poll showed that:

- 1 out of 3 persons reported that alcohol had caused trouble in their families.

- Heavy drinking is involved in 60% of violent crimes, 30% of all suicides, and 80% of fire and drowning accidents.

- The suicide rate of alcoholics is 30 times that of the general population."[23]

Since alcohol is causing such rampant death and destruction, why don't alcohol companies shut down and spare young people all this pain, suffering and death? Why? Because they are making millions of dollars.

In fact, they are so determined to make money, they'll tell you outright lies to keep you drinking. To convince you that drinking is really fun and exciting, they come up with glitzy slogans like "It doesn't get any better than this." The truth is, it doesn't get any **WORSE** than this.

PSYCHIATRIC HOSPITALS

Treating "troubled" teenagers at private institutions is a booming business, costing up to $27,000 a month.

> "A 1985 study showed that over 270,000 kids under 18 were hospitalized that year for psychiatric reasons—more than double the number in 1971.
>
> A great deal of the increase has been in private hospitals, many for profit. And the trend is continuing upward. Even more disturbing is the center's conclusion that *as many as two thirds didn't need to be institutionalized.* "[24]

So why were they locked up? You guessed it.

CINDY'S STORY

Cindy was out of control, so her parents admitted her to a psychiatric hospital. She recalls:

> "They put me on drugs right away. They told me I was depressed, and then they told me I was suicidal. That really threw me..."[25]

Cindy was bombarded with strong medications, and slept up to twenty hours a day. After three months, she showed alarming mood swings and suicidal fantasies. Then, her mother says, the hospital released her, claiming she was doing better.

This sudden "improvement" was discovered right after Cindy's father told the hospital his insurance coverage was about to run out.[26]

There are many fine, private hospitals that provide excellent care for their patients, but unfortunately, many people are only interested in making money. If it means getting you hooked on prescription drugs and locking you up unnecessarily to keep that money rolling in, they'll do it.

The facts are simple. If you are there, they collect. If you leave, they don't.

ABORTION

While debates rage over the abortion issue, one fact screams out loud and clear... abortions bring in **BIG** money. If young girls stopped having them, millions of dollars would be lost.

If you are considering an abortion, keep one thing in mind: if you go through with it, a doctor will make money, a clinic or hospital will make money, nurses will make money, a drug company will make money... a whole system will make money.

But if you decide not to have an abortion, they will *all* lose out. So when someone suggests that you have an abortion, ask yourself, "Who's best interest do they have in mind?"

CAROL EVERETT'S STORY

For six years, Carol Everett was involved in the abortion industry in Texas. Her job was to get into public schools and sell abortions. Here's how she worked:

> "First, I established myself with the teens as an authority on sex. Second, our doctors prescribed low dose birth control pills with a high pregnancy rate... This insured the teens to be my best customers as teenagers typically are not responsible enough to follow such rigid medication guidelines...
>
> I knew their sexual activity would increase... once they were introduced to this contraceptive method. Then I could reach my goal—three to five abortions for each teenager between the ages of 13 and 18."[27]

She continues:

> "We only sold one product— **abortion** —and abortion only. We took what-ever other ideas the pregnant woman had and used them to sell abortion."[28]

Again, you are but a small cog in a big-time, money-making machine. If you believe these people care about what's best for you, you need to wake up. They're looking at what is **most profitable for them.** It's unfortunate that teens like you must suffer, and innocent babies have to die to keep businesses like these flourishing, but that's the way it is.

You may be thinking, "Could people really be that ruthless? Would people really allow horrible things like this to take place just to make money." The Bible gives us the answer:

> "For the love of money is the root of *all evil."*   1 Timothy 6:10

In other words, the ultimate reason for every evil, wicked thing that takes place on this earth is so someone can make a dollar.

LEGAL SYSTEM

Each year parents and others spend many millions of dollars on the legal aspects of teenagers with problems. Attorneys, counsellors, psychiatrists, psychologists and probation officers are but a few of the professionals who profit from teens in trouble.

Then there are the drug treatment programs, alcohol abuse programs, and an endless list of other government and private programs that profit greatly trying to help teens with these problems.

It's interesting: first one group of people gets rich helping teens wreck their life. Then another group steps in and rakes in more cash helping teens undo the problems done by the first group.

It's amazing how much income teens can create for people... as long as they don't do the unthinkable... straighten out their life.

FALSE RELIGIONS

Osho Rajineesh claimed to be a great religious leader, but he was but one more in the long line of phonies who bilk millions of dollars from young people to support their lavish lifestyle, while the young people suffer as a result of the teachings of their leader.

> "At the height of his popularity, Rajineesh amassed 500,000 followers, *87 Rolls-Royces, diamond studded watches, and gowns fashioned from gold thread.*"[29]

The groups annual income from donations "routinely reached millions of dollars."[30]

While Bhagwan admired his fleet of Rolls-Royces and other riches, those who raised the money so he could buy them were paying the ultimate price... their lives.

The same is true of all false religious leaders, who exploit young people so they can enjoy great prosperity. Be careful if you are involved in a religion. Ask yourself, "Am I really serving God, or am I being used to promote the leader's financial empire?"

PORNOGRAPHY

When any group tries to limit young people's access to pornography, those who publish porno squeal like rats trapped in a corner. They have a ready list of arguments to justify publishing their filth...

- **"Freedom of speech!"**

- **"Censorship!"**

- **"You can't prove it's harmful!"**

But those are all smokescreens. They'd never have the guts to admit the real reason they keep pumping it out... it's making them filthy rich.

It would be so refreshing if just once a porno peddler would be honest and admit, "We don't care what effect it has on teens... we want their money." Once more, teens are expendable if it means keeping the business going.

- A 9-year-old boy in Oklahoma had one of his eyes gouged out and his genitals mutilated after he was abducted while walking home from school. A *Hustler* magazine article featured how to do exactly what the abductor did to the little boy.[31]

- While babysitting, a Litchfield, Illinois man stabbed an 11-year-old boy to death and sexually

> molested two girls, 11 and 13.
> When police searched his home,
> they found six pornographic
> magazines. One of the magazines
> included an advertisement about
> sexually molesting children while
> babysitting them.[32]

Page after page could be written, documenting
the harmful effects of pornography on young
people. Hundreds of thousands of teenagers
suffer, either directly or indirectly, because of
it each year.

You may not know it now, but pornography
is a deadly poison, with Satan and his evil
demons crawling all over it. Fortunes are
being made peddling it, but it's at *your*
expense.

And like with many others, those who sell it
are deceived by Satan as well. Someday, they'll
regret they ever had anything to do with it.

PROSTITUTION

A prostitute interviewed on the radio claimed
she earned as much as $14,000 a week.
Imagine what her pimp was making! Do you
think he wants her to quit?

Who cares if she becomes a drug addict to
handle the pain of her lifestyle? Who cares if
she eventually dies of AIDS? There are plenty
more young girls out there who can be lured
in to fill her place.

IMMORAL SEX

We've just discussed pornography and prostitution, but there are millions of dollars more that are generated each year through other immoral sexual activities.

Sexually explicit movies are proven money makers. If the number of rapes and other violent sexual crimes against women rise, the movie's producers can always cry, "You can't prove there's a connection."

No one knows better than Madonna how much money can be made selling sex. As of October, 1993, she was reportedly worth 100 million dollars.[33] But she's just as deceived as those who buy her sleaze. Watch what Satan does to her when he's through using her.

"GAMES"

The makers of Dungeons and Dragons, and other similar "games," have made a fortune off their products. But when teens who play these "games" commit crimes like rape and murder, don't expect the makers of the games to go visit them in jail—or at the cemetery when they die.

DID YOU NOTICE?

Did you notice teen, every subject we talked about in this chapter involved sin... doing something God has told you not to do?

If you simply make up your mind to obey God

and walk with Him, you'll never have to worry about being deceived by these types of people.

God didn't make up His rules to make your life miserable or stop you from having fun. His rules are designed to protect you from people like those you've read about in this chapter.

YOU ARE VALUABLE TO GOD TOO!

You've just seen how valuable you are to a lot of people out there, but you need to know that you are also valuable to God.

For starters, God values you so highly that He sent His only Son to die an agonizing death on the cross, so your sins could be forgiven.

> "In this was manifested (revealed) the love of God toward us, because that God sent his only begotten Son into the world, that we might live through him."   1 John 4:9

Talk about valuable! As a child of God, you are a joint heir with Christ:

> "And if children, then heirs; heirs of God, and *joint heirs with Christ...*"   Romans 8:17

If Jesus lives in your heart, God is building you a mansion in heaven. Jesus Himself gave this wonderful promise:

> "In my Father's house are many mansions: if it were not so, I would

> have told you. *I go to prepare a place for you."*   John 14:2

God values you so highly that He has promised never to leave you:

> "Let your conversation be without covetousness; and be content with such things as ye have: for he hath said, *I will never leave thee, nor forsake thee."*   Hebrews 13:5

WHAT SHOULD I DO?

You don't have to let anyone use you any longer, young person. Because God loves you, He wants to protect you from people who would profit at your expense.

If you will give the Lord control of your life, He will protect you from people the enemy wants to use to destroy you.

10

The Secret About Sex

"We were watching cartoons, then we went to his bedroom," says Xochitl, recalling her first sexual experience, at age 12.

"I knew it was going to happen. We were kissing on the bed, and he went to get a rubber. I wasn't scared. I was excited, 'cause it was him.'"[1]

This is a typical story of a teenager who didn't know the shocking secret about sex that you are about to learn. She thought that if her boyfriend used a condom, she was protected from pregnancy and AIDS.

Hopefully, by the time you finish reading this chapter, you will never make that potentially deadly mistake.

Though the term "safe sex" seems to be the buzzword for the 90's, you need to know that there is only *one* way to practice safe sex, and it's definitely not by using a condom. Because most teens don't know this, the AIDS rate among young people is skyrocketing.

CHRISTIAN TEENS ARE DECEIVED TOO!

Even many Christian teens are believing the "safe sex" lies and are becoming sexually active as a result!

The Christian Broadcasting Network had a Gallup poll done to learn how much impact young people's religious faith had on their sexual behavior.

The results were discouraging. A newspaper article about the study concluded that:

> "Nearly 80% of college students say religion is important in their lives but their faith has relatively little impact on their sexual behavior and attitudes..."[2]

Susan Miller, a senior editor at CBN, said:

> "We were disappointed to see that even though they believe in God, their faith doesn't seem to have much of an effect on their personal

lives and habits, their sexual attitudes and practices."[3]

- **Another study found that 50-60% of evangelical Christian youth are involved in sexual activity.[4]**

- **A survey of 500 church youth found that 62% had participated in oral sex.[5]**

NUMBERS ARE STAGGERING

If you are a sexually active teenager, you can be sure that you are not alone.

"By 1988, 3 out of 4 unmarried 19-year-old women and 5 out of 6 unmarried 19-year-old men were sexually experienced; many had been having sex for several years with several partners..."[6]

A survey revealed that:

"By eighth grade, 61% of the boys and 47% of the girls at the local schools had had sexual intercourse."[7]

BUT I PRACTICE "SAFE SEX!"

I can almost hear a teen screaming out,

"I practice safe sex, so I don't have to worry about any of this!"

Before you make a statement like that, let's see how safe your sex really is. First, we'll examine the reliability of condoms:

CONDOM FAILURE RATE

In a study of homosexual men, the British Medical Journal reported the failure rate due to slippage and breakage at 26%.[8]

That means condoms can fail as often as one out of every four times. Not very safe!

Other studies have come to similar conclusions regarding condoms. Some score their failure rate a little higher, some a little lower.

But the important fact is that condoms are far from perfect. They do fail, and far more often than you may be hearing. And when you are in danger of contracting a deadly disease, a 26% failure rate is far from acceptable.

WHAT ABOUT PREVENTING PREGNANCY?

Condoms fail 15.7% of the time annually in preventing pregnancies.[9]

If you are counting on a condom to prevent you from becoming pregnant, you are playing an extremely risky game.

This is not a popular statement to make, but the facts show that condoms are not as effective at preventing pregnancy as you may think.

"Teenage pregnancies have increased 66% during the past two years at Adams City High School, the *only* school in the Denver metro area to make condoms available to students."[10]

Commenting on the situation, Assistant Principal Carroll Harr stated:

"The bottom line is, what we're doing now *isn't working.*"[11]

WHAT ABOUT DISEASES?

Obviously, if condoms are that ineffective at preventing pregnancies, they are even less effective at preventing you from acquiring sexually transmitted diseases.

WHAT ABOUT AIDS?

If you are counting on condoms to protect you from AIDS, here's the worst news of all. The AIDS virus is so small that it can pass right through a condom. Listen to what one expert in this field says:

"We must recognize that there are other differences between pregnancy prevention and disease prevention. HIV is 1/25th the width of sperm and can pass easily through even the smallest gaps in condoms."[12]

In other words, HIV is so small it can pass right through the microscopic holes in condoms. You may be wondering:

"Then why do all the experts trust

condoms to protect themselves from AIDS?"

The answer is simple... **THEY DON'T!**

They only suggest that you should.

At a conference, 800 sexologists were asked to raise their hand if they would trust a condom to protect them during intercourse with a known HIV-infected person. *Not a single person* raised their hand.[13]

WHO ARE YOU GETTING IN BED WITH?

Since condoms won't protect you from AIDS, you aren't climbing into bed with just that one person. You are actually climbing into bed with every person that person has ever had sex with—and every person any of those people have ever had sex with.

And if *any* of those unknown number of people have the AIDS virus, it could easily be passed on to you.

Experts estimate that millions of people worldwide carry the AIDS virus. And that number is climbing each year at an alarming rate.

Michael Gebott, an Immunologist and AIDS Researcher says:

> "The idea that condoms are going to make it safe for us to continue to live highly promiscuous lives is ridiculous."[14]

OTHER FACTORS

Then there's always the chance that when you are about to have sex, your mind might be so clouded by drugs or alcohol that you may not even think about using a condom.

GINA'S STORY

At 17, Gina's whole life was ahead of her. Like most teens, she dreamed of college, career, marriage and children.

Gina didn't really want to have sex, but felt pressured, so she did. Whenever she tried to get a guy to wear a condom, she got all kinds of attitudes. "What's the matter, don't you trust me?" "Do you think I've got AIDS?" were typical responses.

One night she was out with a guy. She started drinking and lost control of her senses. The next thing she knew they were in bed.

She tried to get him to wear a condom but when he resisted, she was afraid to lose him so she dropped the issue. She says, "the last thing I wanted to do was make him angry."

A few months later Gina tested HIV positive. Now she realizes what a big mistake she made, but it's too late to do anything about it.

"SAFE SEX IS A MYTH"

AIDS Researcher Michael Gebott declares:

> "The whole idea of having safe sex is indeed *a myth.*"[15]

If by chance your condom fails just one time, here are a few consequences you'll likely face:

1. SEXUALLY TRANSMITTED DISEASES

When AIDS came on the scene, some other plagues got lost in the shuffle—venereal diseases.

> "Each year, some *3 million* teenagers contract an STD (Sexually Transmitted Disease);"[16]

That means over 8,500 new teens contract a sexually transmitted disease *every day.*

> "The CDC (Centers For Disease Control) conservatively estimates that every 13 seconds in the United States alone another teenager contracts a sexually transmitted disease, and 6,000 will be infected in the next 24 hours."[17]

Here are a few curses your sex partner might be sharing with you:

• Chlamydia

Chlamydia is a leading cause of infertility, and the most common sexually transmitted disease. There will be four million new cases this year alone.

• Herpes

There's *no cure* for this viral infection that produces painful recurring sores. Some 30 million Americans now have it and a half million more will get it this year.

• Genital Warts

Recently linked to an increased risk of cervical cancer, experts suspect there are more cases of this viral infection in the U. S. than of herpes. It causes warts around the genitals or in the mouth and throat. There is *no cure* for the virus that causes genital warts.[18]

• Syphilis

This bacterial infection can cause brain damage and death. There were 44,000 new cases last year, up almost 70% from five years ago.

> "The syphilis rate among 15-to-19-year-olds jumped *50%* in the 80's.[19]

• Gonorreah

There are more than 700,000 cases in the United States alone. If untreated, gonorreah "can ruin your chances of getting pregnant and can harm your baby if you do."[20]

WHAT ARE MY CHANCES?

> "The C.D.C. reports that **one in four** sexually active teens will contract a venereal disease before finishing high school."[21]

If you are sexually active, you stand a one in four chance of contracting a venereal disease, whether you practice "safe sex" or not.

Young person, before you hop in bed with someone, ask yourself: "Am I willing to risk catching one of these diseases?"

2. UNWANTED PREGNANCY

Another potential consequence of "safe sex" is an unwanted pregnancy. As you have already learned, condoms provide no guarantee of avoiding pregnancy.

> "Each year, *one million* teenage girls, almost one in ten, become pregnant."[22]

If you're a girl, please hear this because far too often, when a girl gets pregnant, the father-to-be moves on, leaving the pregnant girl to face the consequences alone.

> "9% of American girls become mothers before turning 18, and another 9% have abortions."[23]

If you are sexually active, you need to settle one question right now:

"What will I do if I get pregnant?"

You have two choices:

a. Keep the baby: That will mean sacrificing the next 20 years of your life to raise the child. And don't count on your boyfriend for support, regardless of what he promises.

b. Have an abortion: Before you make this choice, you owe it to yourself to thoroughly investigate the abortion issue. Many girls thought they could have an abortion until they learned the graphic details. It's gruesome, but it will open your eyes to the truth.

3. AIDS

C. Everett Coop, the former U.S. Surgeon General said about AIDS:

> "There has never been a disease so tailor made to wipe out an entire generation."[24]

And the generation most likely to be wiped out is today's teenagers:

> "Of the 1 million to 1.5 million HIV-infected Americans, an estimated *one-fifth are teenagers.*"[25]

> "By spring 1989, almost a quarter of the American AIDS population were in their 20's, indicating those people contracted the virus when they were teenagers."[26]

> "In New York City, the biggest killer of women ages 20-29 is AIDS."[27]

That means they are contracting the disease when they are teenagers.

CINDY'S STORY

Cindy dropped out of school at 15, pregnant with her first child. A year later she began smoking marijuana and soon says she had "consumed every drug that's on this earth," including heroin. Eventually she got hooked on crack and had unprotected sex many times to score that drug. Her philosophy was:

> "Who cares about using a condom when all you're trying to do is get a hit?"

When Cindy learned she had AIDS, she began caring. Her children talk about what it will be like when mommy is dead and gone. But the story gets worse. Cindy's 4-year-old daughter was born with AIDS and will also die.[28]

AIDS plays for keeps. Just one condom failure could make you the next Cindy. If your condom is one of the 20% or so that fail, you could be the next AIDS victim.

This is real-life Russian Roulette. Spin the chamber, point the gun to your head and pull the trigger. With condoms, you have a one-in-five chance of blowing your brains out.

Actually, your chances are better with a gun. At least then you have a one-in-six chance.

MELINDA'S STORY

Many teens think their first premarital sexual encounter will be a wonderful and fulfilling experience. But they almost always discover that it's nothing like what they expected.

Melinda went with the same boy for three years, from ages 13 to 16. They had a great relationship. The only problem was that he was always pressuring her to have sex.

When she was 16, Melinda and her boyfriend were alone one evening at her house. Her parents were away on vacation, so they had the house all to themselves. That was the night that her boyfriend finally got to her... and this was the line that did it:

> "You don't have to, but if you really feel in your heart, prove to me that you love me by having sex with me."[29]

After that night, Melinda said, sex was all he ever wanted. She felt used. Soon, he started cheating on her. Before long the relationship dissolved. She looks back now and says:

> "I thought having sex would make our relationship stronger, but in the end, all it did was **destroy it.**"[30]

KATHLEEN'S STORY

Kathleen was 17 when she had a similar first experience with sex. Her friends always made her feel like she was the only girl who hadn't had sex yet. Kathleen remembers:

> "Part of me was tired of being a virgin, and I was sick of being the only one of my friends who hadn't had sex."[31]

One night, Kathleen went to a party at a

friend's house. A guy there was after her all night long. When the party ended, Kathleen decided to spend the night there, so she went upstairs and laid down in bed.

Before long, this guy opened the door and climbed on top of her. Kathleen thought about it for a couple of seconds then decided to go ahead. She recalls how she felt afterward:

> "I regretted my decision from the start... It felt meaningless... It hurt a lot too and he wasn't sensitive to that at all."[31]

But that wasn't all:

> "For the next few days I felt sad... I could hardly eat anything... I lost a lot of respect for myself."[31]

The next time Kathleen saw the young man, she told him how she felt. He responded with:

> "Do you think you are someone special... you're just a girl I slept with."[31]

Undoubtedly, if Kathleen had it to do over again, she would never have done it.

RIGHT SEX

By now you are probably wondering if there is any such thing as real "safe sex." The answer is yes. God instituted sex for married couples... couples of the opposite sex.

> "Let thy fountain be blessed: and
> rejoice with the wife of thy youth.
> Let her be as the loving hind and
> pleasant roe; let her breasts satisfy
> thee at all times; and be thou
> ravished always with her love."
>
> Proverbs 5:18-19

If two teens abstain from all sex until they are married to each other and remain faithful to each other after they are married, only then can they practice truly safe sex.

If you are not willing to make that sacrifice, and insist upon continuing your sexually active lifestyle, ***then you must be prepared to die.***

If you're smart, you'll abstain from sex before you get married. God wants you to enjoy sex, but only with your husband or wife:

> "Marriage is honourable in all, and
> the bed undefiled: but whoremongers
> and adulterers God will judge."
>
> Hebrews 13:4

God doesn't forbid sex before marriage because He wants to be mean. He forbids it because He knows it will harm you. And since He loves you, He made rules to protect you. That's real love.

Would a loving parent allow their child to play in a busy street because the child enjoys it?

Of course not! For the sake of their child's safety, parents force their child to forfeit a little pleasure to ensure a longer life.

In the same way, God commands you to forfeit immoral sex because He knows it's not worth the awful price you will have to pay. All God's rules are for your own good.

Please don't let the devil's world system deceive you any longer. If you have been sexually active in the past, stop right now.

If you are a virgin, stay that way until God brings the person into your life that He wants you to marry. Don't let anyone shame or embarrass you into becoming sexually active. It's not worth it.

If you do abstain, someday you will enjoy a lifetime of sex with your spouse, without fear of venereal diseases or AIDS.

WHY ALL THE FALSE INFORMATION?

You may be wondering, "If all this is true, why aren't more people out there telling us the truth? There are several reasons:

1. Many people honestly don't know the truth. They are well-meaning people who learned the "safe sex" myth from experts and passed along to you what they were taught.

2. Other people don't want you to know the truth because they would lose a lot of money.

3. Many politicians don't dare say anything that would anger the homosexual community. It could very well ruin their chances of getting elected again.

There are many reasons the truth isn't being shared a lot, but thank God, now you know that the whole "safe sex" campaign is a fraud.

Nothing is "safe" when you disobey God.

11

The Secret About Satanism

A 48-year-old California woman sat in a courtroom and told her horrifying story.

She said her parents forced her to participate in gruesome satanic rituals as a child. One of those rituals included stabbing to death her own infant daughter. The woman confessed:

> "I was supposed to cut and kill her and I couldn't do it and I dropped the knife."[1]

She then testified that she finally killed the child after being drugged and having electric probes placed in her neck.

She said that her father then cut up the infant and burned the tiny body, chanting,

"Satan's baby into Satan's fire."[2]

Satanism, though presented as a harmless "no-strings-attached" way for young people to receive power, money, drugs, sex, etc., is actually the worship of the most evil creature ever created... Lucifer himself.

And all those "goodies" are just bait Satan uses to entrap victims in his deadly web.

Because of this deception, multiplied thousands of teenagers are diving headlong into occult activity, never learning how dangerous it is until they are in way too deep.

NANCY'S STORY

Nancy admitted to a radio talk show host that she had been addicted to cocaine for two years. When the host asked her where she got the money for the drugs, she replied:

> "Well, most of the time I get the drugs for free. I know some guys involved in satanism. When I need some drugs, they come around. They take me places and get me stoned so I'll perform sexually for them."

"What kind of places?"

"Where they hold ceremonies."

"What kind of ceremonies?"

"Animal... and human," she blurted out.

"When was the last time you saw them kill someone?"

"The first time, it was an infant. Two weeks ago, they sacrificed a six-year-old child. Afterwards, they warned me they'd sacrifice me too if I ever told anyone."[3]

What a tragedy! In the beginning, Nancy thought this was a great deal. All the drugs she could take—**FREE!** Who could beat that? Eventually, though, she learned that the drugs were just a tool the satanists used to abuse her sexually—and to lure her into the depths of satanism.

Now it was time to start paying for those drugs. Nancy's eyes bulged in horror as she watched a knife-wielding, black-robed figure murder an innocent six-year-old child.

By the time Nancy learned the secret about satanism, she had seen too much. She was threatened that if she told anyone or tried to leave, she would be the next sacrifice.

I WANT YOU!

The rock group *Piledriver* sings a song about the true desires of their master, Satan:

**"I just want to rule your mind...
Now I'm your god, and I'm your lord"**

What should alarm you is that those who are already involved in this deadly religion want to entangle *you* in it too!

What makes satanism even more dangerous is that satanists are professional liars. In fact, their father, Satan, is the father of lies:

> "Ye are of your father the devil, and the lusts of your father ye will do. He (Satan) was a murderer from the beginning, and abode not in the truth, because there is no truth in him. When he speaketh a lie, he speaketh of his own: *for he is a liar, and the father of it.*"   John 8:44

So it shouldn't surprise you that those who worship Satan would readily lie to recruit new members or to cover their illegal activities.

CHRISTIAN TEENS ARE BEING DECEIVED TOO!

It's not just unsaved teens who are being deceived into involvement in satanism. Many Christian teens are falling prey to the devil's tactics and becoming active in local covens.

AMANDA'S STORY

Amanda's father pastors a soul winning, evangelistic church in the Bible belt down south. Amanda was raised in a Christian home and grew up in the church. If anyone should have been wise to the devil's tactics, it should have been her. But even she fell into deception.

Though no one (including her parents) knew about it, Amanda confided in a friend that she had been deceived by the kind acts of "nice" people.

At first, the activities seemed like harmless fun. But once she was trapped, the ropes began tightening themself around her. Then, before she knew it, she was active in a satanic coven!

Eventually, this child of God was forced to witness some of the cruelest acts imaginable.

WE'RE NICE PEOPLE... HONEST!

A television interview with Zeena LaVey, who was representing the Church of Satan, is a great example of their tactics. Zeena is the daughter of Anton LaVey, founder of the Church of Satan and author of *The Satanic Bible.*

The interview was part of a massive Public Relations campaign Satanists are mounting to change their image, which will make recruiting efforts easier and more effective.

During the interview, Zeena insisted that satanists are wonderful, peace-loving people who are greatly misunderstood. She contended that they are victims of prejudice and are being wrongly persecuted for their harmless religious beliefs.

The main problem, she felt, was that people really don't understand them. She came across sweet and gentle. I'm sure that many young people were swayed in their perception of satanism because of her performance.

But in truth, satanism is nothing like what Zeena portrayed. Their Public Relations blitz is designed to eliminate any fears you might have about satanism so that when someone approaches you about getting involved, you won't be afraid to give it a try.

THE TRUTH LEAKS OUT

Satanist Michael Aquino reveals a principle that is crucial to satanists:

> "The governing principle of magick is the ability to **control people without their realizing how or why they're being controlled.**"[4]

That's the essence of satanism. Controlling young people and leading them down the road to destruction without them knowing they are being led.

SOME FACTS SHE DIDN'T MENTION

Unfortunately, Zeena skipped a few important facts. Her father, Anton LaVey, wrote 11 Satanic Rules of the Earth. Rule #11 says:

> "When walking in open territory, bother no one. If someone bothers you, ask him to stop. If he does not stop, ***destroy him.***"5

That doesn't sound very peace-loving to me. Anton LaVey also said:

> "All men are created equal, some are just more equal than others. ***Some should be eliminated.***"6

Zeena also never mentioned that her boyfriend at the time was Nicholas Schreck, a former member of the Manson family.[7]

BEYOND THE HYPE

Satanism is a dangerous religion. The devil's servants will say ***anything*** to entrap you. Please don't believe them. Instead, look at those who've already made that mistake:

MAN BUTCHERS 3-YEAR-OLD GIRL

The headline read, ***"Man says he killed for Satan."*** A 21-year-old Fullerton, California man attacked a 3-year-old girl who was asleep in her bedroom, sexually molested her, then repeatedly stabbed her until she was dead.

How could anyone do such a demented and sick thing? In a jailhouse interview, Michael Pacewitz confessed that:

> ***"The devil wanted me to do it*** and I wanted to do it for him."[8]

What's worse, he showed absolutely no remorse over the senseless butchering of this innocent young girl. Pacewitz continues:

> "I'm not sorry because I wanted to do it. *I wanted her dead.*"⁹

No, Michael, *you* didn't want her dead. The demons who drove you to commit this horrible crime are the ones who wanted her dead. They want *every* innocent child dead.

After murdering the girl, Pacewitz surrendered to police. He was in a phone booth, clutching a large knife with dried blood on it. Pacewitz said he thought about killing the girl for three hours before stabbing her.

THEY'RE NOT OF US!

When confronted with hideous accounts like this, those in the occult always respond with excuses like:

- **People like that have nothing to do with satanism.**
- **They're radicals who are trying to give us a bad name.**
- **They're just mentally sick people.**

A few probably are mentally sick people with no ties to satanism, but not all of them.

Literally thousands of people worldwide are reporting strikingly similar stories about satanic activity they have witnessed personally.

MURDERS IN MEXICO

Let's venture into the heart of real-life Satan worship to see first-hand what it's like. First stop—Matamoros, Mexico, sight of several ghastly Satanic human sacrifices.

Carlos Tapia, Chief Deputy of Cameron County, Texas, which is right across the border from Matamoros, describes the scene:

> "You could smell the stench... blood and decomposing organs. In a big, cast iron pot there were pieces of human bodies and a goat's head with horns."[10]

Why would anyone do something so vile? Tapia continues:

> "They believed that by sacrificing innocent human beings, their loads of marijuana would have an invisible shield of protection from law enforcement officials."[11]

Here's what they did to a private investigator who was working for the father of one of the murdered boys:

> "They cut the skin off the bottoms of both his feet and made him walk on salt. Then they put him in a tub of water and boiled him alive. While he was screaming, they pulled pieces of raw flesh off his body."[12]

Jim Mattox, the Texas State Attorney General in charge of the investigation of the Matamoros cult crimes, said:

> *"I believe that the devil possessed these murderers."*[13]

The mother of one of the murdered boys said:

> "I think the suspects *must be possessed by the devil."*[14]

TWO GIRLS ABUSED IN SATANIC RITUALS

Two girls from Maine, ages 13 and 14, were removed from their homes by authorities because they were so badly abused in satanic rituals. One of the girls remembers:

> "The police who came to the door found two beaten children, each weighing less than 70 pounds. They only saw the tip of the iceberg. They didn't see how bad the beatings really were, nor the sexual abuse, *nor the satanic rituals..."*[15]

"I'D KILL INSTANTLY!"

A young man who called a radio talk show claimed to be a satanist. When asked if he would kill for Satan, he replied, "I'd kill instantly." Then the boy asked the radio host:

> "Have you ever tasted blood? Have you ever run your hands through warm guts?"

The young man was taken off the air and later confessed that he was teaching his 6-year-old daughter to sacrifice animals and taste their blood."[16]

This is what satanism is *really* like. And there are thousands more similar stories. Police units that deal with satanic crimes report untold numbers of these incidents.

Hopefully, though, you now see that satanism is *not* a peace-loving religion that cares about the good of man. It's the worship of Satan, the most blood-thirsty creature ever created—one who demands the torture and mutilation of as many people and animals as possible.

WHERE SATANISM ENDS

As was already mentioned, satanism begins with promises of power, drugs, friends, sex, money—whatever you want.

Here are the stories of a few teens who believed those recruiting promises and enlisted. Let's see how they fared after serving Satan.

SLIT HIS MOTHER'S THROAT

Fourteen-year-old Tommy Sullivan was a devout Roman Catholic until he descended into satanism. Once he became totally deceived, he promised to kill for Satan, which he did.

He slit his mother's throat and made dozens of slashes with the thrust of a knife. He tried to gouge her eyes out, and partially severed her hands.

The next day he was found dead, his wrists were cut and his throat slashed from ear to ear, nearly decapitating him. [17]

DEREK'S STORY

Derek told his girlfriend that Satan had visited him, and had demanded his soul. Derek then took his stepfather's hunting rifle to his basement bedroom, crammed the gun barrel into his mouth and pulled the trigger.[18]

Teen, Satan is the father of deception. He and his evil servants will promise you anything. You may even receive a few of those desires for awhile, but sooner or later, you will realize that you have been horribly deceived and will wish you had never listened to him.

THE ULTIMATE PURPOSE

If you are a Christian, the devil will destroy your testimony and make you worthless as a servant of Christ. More than one Christian teen has been tricked into participating in coven activities. Now they live in terror— fearing they can't escape Satan's clutches.

If you are not a Christian, then Satan wants you to worship him so you won't worship the true God. The reason Satan fell in the first place was because he wanted worship that only the true God deserves.

As long as he can keep you worshipping him, he can torture and abuse you, and keep you away from the freedom that only Jesus Christ can give you.

Satan's ultimate goal is to see you thrown into the eternal flames of hell. He'll promise you anything, but that is what he really wants for you.

Please turn away from his lies and reject his false religion. There's no denying that it can be extremely tempting to get involved in satanism. That's why so many teens are getting hooked.

But if you look beyond the promises and see what satanism actually delivers, you'll agree that what you may receive is not worth the price you will surely have to pay.

THE WHITE WITCHCRAFT LIE

While we are on the subject of satanism and it's deception, there's another lie the devil wants to deceive you with.

Many young people are being recruited into satanism through an extremely deceptive trick. Satan knows that some young people can be lured into satanism through promises of power, money and sex, even if it means being evil in return.

But other teens would run if they thought it was evil. Since Satan wants **EVERY** young person and adult to burn in hell, he developed a plan to drag in teens who want nothing to do with evil. It's called "white witchcraft."

IS WHITE WITCHCRAFT REALLY WHITE?

People are popping up everywhere declaring that they are "white" witches or Wiccans. They say they have nothing to do with satanism, and only use their powers to help people.

A typical example is this Wiccan from Virginia. A newspaper article about her says:

> "Cheryl St. John doesn't cast evil spells. She'd rather bake chocolate raisin bread than stir eye of newt and toe of frog into a bubbling cauldron."[19]

That sounds innocent enough, doesn't it? Cheryl says:

> "Most of our people use magic to heal themselves and bring what we need into our lives. There are a lot of wackos out there, but we're as ethical a bunch of people as you're ever going to meet. Our basic law is 'do as you will, but harm none.'"[20]

All this propaganda sounds great until you realize it's all coming from the same father of lies, Satan. Please don't be deceived. There is nothing good about any of it. There cannot possibly be such a thing as "good witchcraft" because **ALL** witchcraft is 100% evil.

If anyone would know if both "black" and "white" witchcraft existed, Anton LaVey would. In *The Satanic Bible,* he declares:

> "White magic is supposedly utilized only for good or unselfish purposes, and black magic, we are told, is used only for selfish or 'evil' reasons. ***Satanism draws no dividing line.***"21

In *The Satanic Bible* he also says:

> "There is ***no difference between 'White' and 'Black' magic,*** except in the smug hypocrisy, guilt ridden righteousness, and ***self-deceit*** of the 'White' magician himself."22

In Anton LaVey's own words, he says there is no difference between Black and White witchcraft. Any White magician who tells you there is a difference is either lying or is living in "self-deceit."

In short, "white" witchcraft is nothing more than a tool Satan uses to take the fear out of becoming involved in literal satanism. By the time you discover that you've been lied to, you might be in serious trouble.

Teen, satanism is a dangerous and bloody religion, no matter what name it goes by. The consequences of getting involved are severe. Please don't be deceived by the lies. Stay away from satanism.

12

The Secret About the Voices in Your Head

While kneeling naked by his bed praying to Satan for the first time, Sean heard an audible voice say, "I love you." He opened his eyes to see who had entered his room but, to his shock, *no one was there.*

This event took place when Sean was a teenager. A girl he knew had recruited him into satanism, promising him power.

Excitement grew within Sean as he realized that he had tapped into the supernatural. He was sure that these voices would lead him where he wanted to go.

Instead, they took him into deeper and deeper

bondage to Satan. What Sean didn't know was that his involvement in satanism had opened the doors for demons to enter his body and take control of his life.

Once under Satan's control, the demons drove Sean to carry a gun to a local convenience store one night, where he brutally shot the store clerk to death.

But Satan wasn't through using this poor, deceived young person yet. Six months later, Sean snuck into his parent's bedroom as they lay asleep in bed and shot them both to death.

Eventually, Sean learned the secret that the voices he had been hearing were actually demons inside of him.

WHERE ARE THESE VOICES COMING FROM?

Many teenagers are hearing voices in their head that nobody else can hear. And a growing number of young people who are committing senseless murders contend that these voices are instructing them to kill others, or even take their own life

Here are some lyrics by another guy who says he hears these voices, Ozzy Osbourne, from his song, "Shot In The Dark":

**"Voices are calling from inside
    my head
I can hear them, I can hear them..."**

Now those same demonic voices are coming through Ozzy's music, bringing deception and ruin to many unsuspecting teenagers. A 14-year-old girl delivers this frightening report:

> "One night after listening to Ozbourne's music *I started hearing a voice calling me.* It was real scary... I play heavy metal daily. I try to stop but I can't. It's like *someone inside of me* telling me to do wrong things...
>
> I sometimes feel like killing myself... I feel as if I am two people, one is good and one is bad and somehow the bad is overpowering the good."[1]

Teen, if you are hearing voices like this, you can be sure that demons have somehow gained entrance to your body and are talking to you.

JIM GORDON'S STORY

Jim Gordon was a famous rock drummer. He played for stars like John Lennon, George Harrison, Eric Clapton, Jackson Browne and many others. But when he began hearing demonic voices his whole life changed.

Here's how Rolling Stone magazine tells it:

> "On June 3rd, 1983, there was nothing on his mind except killing his mother. *The voices told him what to do next.* One said to

hit her with a hammer first, so she would not suffer when he stabbed her with the knife. He would obey..."[2]

CRAIG'S STORY

Craig began hearing voices after he started playing Dungeons and Dragons. He obeyed the voices, thinking that since he had reached the supernatural realm, he had an edge up on the rest of the world.

As time passed, the voices led him into powerful satanic bondage. When he felt trapped and wanted out, the voices threatened to kill him and his family unless he obeyed.

Craig learned that through playing occult games like D & D, he had opened himself up for demons to come into his body. Now they were terrorizing him.

PRINCE HEARS VOICES

The million dollar question in rock circles was why did the rock star formerly known as Prince mysteriously change his name to an unusual symbol. His answer was:

"I followed the advice of my spirit."[3]

In other words, a demon told him to. Whether he realizes it or not, obeying those demonic voices will lead this famous musician straight to destruction.

FIELD OF LIES!

Remember the movie "Field of Dreams"? Voices in the farmer's head kept telling him what to do. As he obeyed, all the pieces fell into place, and in a tear-jerking finale, his life-long dream was fulfilled—he got to meet his dad.

The movie's message was simple—obey the voices in your head and everything will work out for you, too!

Don't be deceived! That's a bold faced satanic lie. If you listen to and obey unseen voices, it will lead you to destruction. Nothing turns out good when you listen to demons.

MUSIC LEADS TO VOICES

An all-too typical teenage boy reported that after listening to certain Heavy Metal music tapes every day, voices started talking to him in his head.

He said it was like the voices forced him to do bad things. They even made him feel like killing himself. Sin and destruction are *always* the desire of demons.

An alarming number of teens are learning from experience that involvement in any satanically controlled activities, like Heavy Metal, Ouija boards, satanism, astrology, etc. can allow demons to enter your body and speak to you.

Be very careful what you get involved in.

If you participate in anything satanic, whether it seems innocent or not, you will open yourself up to being infested by demons.

ROCK STARS ADMIT BEING INFESTED

Part of the price rock stars must pay for their fame is having demons (knowingly or unknowingly) live inside them and control them.

Marc Storace, lead vocalist for *Krokus,* says:

> "You can't describe it except to say it's like a mysterious energy that comes *into my body.* It's almost like being a medium."[4]

He continues:

> "If you *allow them entrance,* if you allow yourself to meditate with the dark powers... people will respond to them."[5]

A friend of rock god Jim Hendrix stated:

> "He (Jimi) believed that he was *possessed by some spirit,* and I got to believe it myself... he really believed it and was wrestling with it constantly."[6]

One of Jimi's girlfriends, Fayne Pridgon, was also aware of his problem:

> "He used to talk about *some devil or something was IN him.* He used to talk about us going... and having

some root lady or somebody see if she could drive this demon out of him."[7]

As we all know, the demons drove Jimi to an eternity in hell before he had a chance to be set free.

Some lyrics from the song "Suicidal Maniac" by the group "Suicidal Tendencies" have this to say about Satan and his demons:

"I bow to his might
Too powerful to fight
It's my destiny
Now the Maniac *lives inside of me.*"

Many other rock stars readily admit that demons live inside of them and communicate with them.

Former Beatle John Lennon didn't write his own songs. Demons gave them to him and he just wrote them down:

"When the real music comes to me... that has nothing to do with me, 'cause *I'm just a channel.* The only joy for me is for it to be given to me, and to transcribe it *like a medium...*"[8]

John Lennon also learned that Satan doesn't treat his servants very well. He was shot down in cold blood in front of his New York City apartment.

WHAT SHOULD I DO?

If unseen voices are pressuring you to do bad things, then you need to understand that demons live inside of you and are talking to you.

Here are a few suggestions:

1. Recognize that you are dealing with real demons, and that their ultimate desire is to control you, then destroy you. It is **NOT** God talking to you.

2. Accept Jesus Christ as your personal Savior if you haven't already done so. Without Christ in your life, you are powerless against Satan's evil forces.

3. Confess and forsake any and all sin that the Holy Spirit brings to your mind. Ask God to forgive you for any involvement in anything belonging to Satan. Then turn your back on all of it and submit control of your life to God.

4. Burn anything you have that is associated with the occult or the New Age Movement. (Occultic rock music albums, tapes, C.D.'s, occult jewelry, rock posters, Ouija boards, etc. That's what they did in Bible days:

> "And many of them also which used curious arts brought their books together, *and burned them* before all men..."   Acts 19:19

5. **Ask the Lord** in prayer to lead you to

someone who has knowledge and experience in the field of deliverance.

YOU CAN BE SET FREE

The most exciting news of all is that, through the power of Jesus Christ, the demons can be kicked out of you and you can be set free.

> "If the Son (Jesus) therefore shall make you free, ye shall be free indeed."   John 8:36

When Jesus walked the earth He kicked demons out of many people. And He's still doing it today.

> "When the even was come, they brought unto (Jesus) many that were possessed with devils (demons): and *he cast out the spirits with his word,* and healed all that were sick:"   Matthew 8:16

> "Then was brought unto (Jesus) one possessed with a devil (demon), blind, and dumb: *and he healed him,* insomuch that the blind and dumb both spake and saw."
>
>   Matthew 12:22

When demons tell you there's no way out, or that you can't escape, they are lying. Jesus Christ *can* and *will* set you free.

13

The Secret About Homosexuality

LAUREN WAS A 16-YEAR-OLD VIRGIN.

Long ago, she came up with three reasons why she wouldn't have sex until after she was married.

She didn't want to get a sexually transmitted disease. She definitely didn't want to get pregnant. And most of all, she was scared to death of getting AIDS.

But one day at school Lauren found herself in a class learning about "safe sex." Her teacher assured her that by using a condom she and her boyfriend could enjoy the pleasure of sex with none of the worries she'd always held.

After the class, the teacher handed Lauren a condom on her way out. She quickly stuffed it in her purse and raced down the hall to her next class.

For the next several weeks, Lauren heard an endless list of reasons why "safe sex" was the perfect answer. The fears she once had were slowly being replaced with excitement and anticipation at the thought of having an active and safe sex life with her boyfriend.

After a few of these classes, Lauren began getting the impression that *everyone* was having sex. She felt like she was the only one "missing out."

One Friday night, Lauren drove over to her boyfriend's. His parents were out of town so they were alone in the house.

As they sat together on the sofa, Lauren's fears all melted away as she recalled the lessons from the "safe sex" classes. She then slipped her hand into her purse and gripped the condom. It made her feel very secure.

That night, Lauren and her boyfriend had sex for the first time. Lauren felt so free and was thankful for those "safe sex" classes. No longer did she have to worry about the lectures her parents were always giving her about premarital sex. Now she and her boyfriend could have sex whenever they wanted.

THE UNEXPECTED HAPPENS

About six months later, Lauren caught a cold. As the days passed, rather than getting better, her condition grew worse. Eventually she went to her doctor for a physical and several tests. The next week, Lauren returned to the doctor's office for the results.

THIS CAN'T BE TRUE!

As warmly and softly as he could, Lauren's doctor informed her that she had tested positive for HIV.

"THAT'S IMPOSSIBLE!" Lauren screamed!

"I've only had sex with one person and we ALWAYS used a condom!" she insisted. Lauren's boyfriend, who was in another office, came in and made a confession.

"I'm HIV positive too," he told her, choking back the tears.

"I've been HIV positive all the time we've been seeing each other. But I didn't say anything because I thought the condoms would protect you. I'm sorry."

Then Lauren's doctor told her something that no one had ever taught her in any of her "safe sex" classes.

"Lauren, condoms don't stop the HIV virus. That virus is so small it passes right through the holes in condoms."

Lauren was in shock! She thought, "This can't be happening to me!"

Within two years, Lauren's sickness became severe. Her pain increased and her strength decreased. While bedridden and in constant pain, Lauren cursed the day she believed what she had been taught in school. One year later, she was dead.

Lauren is just one of millions of teens who are already infected with the HIV virus. Thousands more are being infected every day:

> "The number of AIDS cases among teens *"doubles every 14 months."*[1]

And believe it or not,:

> "AIDS cases among teens and young adults grew **77%** in the past two years."[2]

WHERE IS IT ALL COMING FROM?

The bulk of all "safe sex" preaching is coming from the homosexual community. Though they claim their only desire is to teach young people about AIDS awareness and prevention, their "safe sex" campaign is really a smokescreen, hiding their hidden agenda, an agenda they really don't want you to know about.

Before beginning, though, please understand that this information is not designed to attack homosexuals. I do not hate homosexuals. I wish homosexuals no harm. In fact, my desire is that homosexuals will learn that, though Jesus hates the sin of homosexuality, He loves them and wants to set them free from this sin that has them in bondage.

THE AGENDA

In fairness to you, though, I must expose their hidden agenda so you can make intelligent decisions about this life and death issue. It wouldn't be fair for you to learn that there is no such thing as "safe sex" the same way Lauren did.

Often, when these topics are discussed in public schools, students are told not to tell their parents what is said in class. That should tip you off that they don't want to **teach** you, they want to *convert you*. They're afraid you might learn some facts they don't want you to know.

You need to understand that the homosexual community has two main goals:

1. To make sure that nobody interferes with their lifestyle or tries to stop them from having homosexual sex.

2. To brainwash everyone into believing that homosexuality is a normal alternate lifestyle.

To accomplish these goals, they are bombarding young people on every front. Movies like the pro-homosexual *Philadelphia,* plus many television movies that have homosexual themes are being produced. Homosexuals are working their way into all grades of public schools to spread their message.

In addition, they are using tons of printed literature, plus rallies, marches, speeches and lectures to convince young people that homosexuality is a normal alternate lifestyle.

To prove that it isn't, I was planning to describe some activities homosexuals engage in. However, God showed me this scripture:

> "And have no fellowship with the unfruitful works of darkness, but rather reprove them. *For it is a shame even to speak of those things which are done of them in secret."*   Ephesians 5:11-12

So I will leave it up to you to investigate if you wish. It is enough to say that their practices are repulsive beyond imagination.

THE BIG PROBLEM

When AIDS came along, the homosexual community was faced with a real problem. The only two solutions were to stop having homosexual sex or convince people that AIDS could be prevented by having "safe sex."

Since homosexuals are driven by satanic forces to engage in perverted sex, they *cannot* stop on their own. Therefore they will say or do anything to justify their lifestyle.

So their only alternative was to convince people that there was a way to have "safe sex" without fear of AIDS. That's the purpose of all their propaganda.

Their main concern is *not* to help you have "safe sex," they want to justify their lifestyle so they can keep feeding the lusts of their flesh.

With each passing day, they are becoming more bold in their attempts to justify that lifestyle. Many have reached the point where they proudly proclaim that even God Himself approves of homosexuality.

IS GOD REALLY FOR IT?

One homosexual seminary student says:

> "I felt a strong call and gift from God for the ministry (and) I found I had just as strong a call and gift from God for being gay..."[3]

Homosexual "minister" Troy Perry, founder of Metropolitan Community Church:

> "Metropolitan Community Church started out of a revelation that God gave me that God loves gay people. We now have over 267 churches in eleven countries preaching the good news of Jesus Christ to gays and lesbians that God loves them and they can be the people God wants them to be."[4]

The homosexual movement has convinced many people that God endorses their lifestyle. Some religious denominations now ordain homosexuals and lesbians as ministers.

So-called "experts" declare that they have conclusive scientific evidence proving that homosexuality is not a matter of choice... they claim they are born homosexual. One homosexual proudly boasts:

> "I didn't make me 'gay.' **God made me 'gay.'**"[5]

Rev. Thomas Bigalo, a homosexual activist, said:

> "Homosexuality is no different than having brown eyes. It's the way you're made."[6]

Is this true? Does God really create people as homosexuals? According to *Human Sexuality,* a textbook written by Masters, Johnson and Kolodny:

> "There is **no credible scientific evidence** to support homosexual claims that 'gayness' is either genetically determined or im-mutable. The genetic theory of homosexuality has been generally discarded today,"[7]

The same book continues:

> "Despite the interest in possible

> hormone mechanisms in the origin of homosexuality, no serious scientist today suggests that a simple cause-effect relationship applies."[8]

Don't be deceived, teen. Homosexuals are not born that way. It's just another excuse to justify their behavior.

Next we must ask, "Is God REALLY for it?" "Rev." Perry said at a homosexual rally:

> "The only people who discriminate against us are people who usually are very ignorant on the subject *and haven't read scripture.*"[9]

"Rev" Perry is hoping that you won't check him out on this, but that's exactly what we're going to do. Let's go to the scriptures and see what God says:

> "Thou shalt not lie with mankind, as with womankind: *it is abomi-nation."*   Leviticus 18:22

The word "abomination" means that God feels extreme disgust and hatred for this sin. But though He hates the sin, He still loves the sinner. God loves homosexuals, He just wants them to repent of their sin.

Later, God repeats His feelings on the subject. This time he declares the penalty for those who practice this sin:

> "If a man also lie with mankind, as he lieth with a woman, both of them have committed an abomination: *they shall surely be put to death.*"   Leviticus 20:13

If God created people as homosexuals and approved of that lifestyle, He would *never* have commanded that they be put to death.

Here are two verses from the New Testament. Do they sound like God has changed His mind?:

> "For this cause God gave them (homosexuals and lesbians) up unto *vile (wicked)* affections: for even their women did change the natural use into that which is against nature:
>
> And likewise also the men, leaving the natural use of the woman, burned in their lust one toward another; men with men working that which is *unseemly (indecent, shameful),* and receiving in themselves that recompence of their error which was meet."
>   Romans 1:26-27

No matter what anyone tells you, here's proof that God does **NOT** approve of homosexuality. Throughout the Bible, the Lord proclaims His hatred for this deviate sexual practice.

But in their attempt to justify their lifestyles, homosexuals twist and pervert the Bible to make it say what they want it to say.

A former homosexual who was saved by the blood of Jesus and rescued from that lifestyle talks about what it was like back when he was still a homosexual:

> "We had to twist the scriptures in order to justify our lifestyle. We literally created our own theology. Today the homosexual movement is pressuring traditional churches to do the same." [10]

Another former homosexual comes to the same conclusion:

> "I've never seen more cunning twisting of the scriptures than in the 'Gay' theology." [11]

Please understand that **NONE** of this is my opinion. This is what God Almighty has declared in His Word to be the truth:

> "Sanctify them through thy truth: *thy word is truth.*"   John 17:17

God issues yet another warning on the subject:

> "Know ye not that the unrighteous shall not inherit the kingdom of God? Be not deceived: neither fornicators... *nor effeminate, nor*

> ***abusers of themselves with mankind***... shall inherit the kingdom of God."   1 Corinthians 6:9-10

Again, you can be sure that if God approved of the homosexual lifestyle, He would never condemn to hell those who practice it.

As was mentioned at the start of this chapter, this is not intended to attack homosexuals. However, when they begin demanding that others accept their sexual lifestyle as normal, they need to learn that it isn't normal.

When they start telling you lies that could cost you your life, someone must give you the facts. You deserve to know the truth.

WHAT ARE THEY REALLY LIKE?

Are homosexuals really soft-spoken, loving people, as they would like you to believe? Or are they militant and demanding?

In a speech before nearly 300,000 homosexuals and lesbians in Washington D.C., homosexual activist Duke Comedes screamed the following words to a roaring audience:

> "Get ready America, we are coming forward in ever increasing numbers. We have become a tide of strength. ***Do NOT stand in our way.***"[12]

Lesbian activist leader Robin Tyler screamed the following message to the same crowd:

> "We are here to tell you that it is
> **YOU** who should now be afraid of
> **US.** Do you understand that you
> have backed us into a corner and
> that we are ready, willing and able
> to come out fighting. We are mad as
> hell and we are not going to take it
> anymore." [13]

In short, the homosexual community will do
almost anything it takes to continue in their
sin. Those who refuse to agree with them and
accept their lifestyle as normal are considered
the enemy. Here are a few activities that
militant homosexuals advocate:

1. Blood terrorism

At the same rally, Robert Swab, homosexual
activist and former President of the Texas
Human Rights Foundation threatened:

> "If research money for AIDS is not
> coming at a certain level by a certain
> date, all gay males should give
> blood. Whatever action is required
> to get national attention is valid. *If
> that includes blood terrorism, so
> be it.* "[14]

If they really wanted to stop the spread of
AIDS, why not stop their high risk behavior—
homosexual sex. But because they are under
the control of the demonic spirits that drive
them, they would never consider such a thing.

Instead, they demand that we finance finding a cure for them while they continue their high risk behavior, and threaten to kill us if we don't put forth enough effort.

2. Repeal Sodomy Laws

The repealing of sodomy laws would allow parents to homosexually molest their children, or other innocent children legally.

Because of AIDS, a growing number of homosexuals are turning to children to satisfy their craving for perverted sex. NAMBLA (North American Man/Boy Love Association) is seeking to legalize sex between adults and children.

Their ultimate goal is to remove the age of consent law altogether. They maintain that if adults could have sex with children, the adults chances of getting AIDS would be greatly reduced. Maybe so, but what about the poor child's chances of getting AIDS?.

Homosexuals are so driven by demons to continue their unnatural sex, their only concern is that no one be allowed to stop them, even if it means giving children AIDS.

Listen to this chilling quote from homosexual activist Michael Swift which was printed in the *Gay Community News*:

> "We shall sodomize your sons, emblems of your feeble masculinity...

> We shall seduce them in your schools, in your dormitories, in your gymnasiums, in your locker rooms, in your sports arenas, in your seminaries, in your youth groups."[15]

Mr. Swift continues:

> "We will triumph only when we present a common face to the vicious heterosexual enemy. If you dare to cry faggot, fairy, queer, at us, we will stab you in your cowardly hearts and *defile your dead, puny bodies.*"[16]

It's ironic that he would mention *defiling bodies.* God condemns those who do just that:

> "Knowing this, that the law is not made for a righteous man, but for the lawless and disobedient... for whoremongers, *for them that defile themselves with mankind...*"
>
> 1 Timothy 1:9-10

3. Throwing bombs

Larry Cramer, a homosexual and an internationally known playwright, says that as homosexuals:

> "We have to scare people! We should throw bombs! We should set fires!"[17]

4. Murdering anyone who opposes them.

Michael Swift also wrote in the *Gay Community News*:

> "All churches who oppose us will be closed. Our only gods are handsome young men. We adhere to a cult of beauty, moral and esthetic. All that is ugly and vulgar and banal **will be annihilated...**

> "We shall be victorious because we are fueled with the ferocious bitterness of the oppressed who have been forced to play seemingly bit parts in your dumb hetero-sexual shows throughout the ages. **We too are capable of firing guns.**"[18]

While marching down a Washington D.C. street, mobs of homosexuals gestured with their hands as though they were firing a pistol, while chanting the words, "Bigots gotta go... Bigots gotta go..."

To militant homosexuals, a "bigot" is anyone who refuses to believe what the homosexual community demands that they believe.

Yet these poor deceived men don't realize that God Himself is among those who condemn their sexual lifestyle:

> "Even as Sodom and Gomorrha,

and the cities about them in like manner, giving themselves over to fornication, and going after strange flesh, are set forth for an example, *suffering the vengeance of eternal fire."*   Jude 7

THERE IS HOPE

Despite the wickedness of this sin, there is hope for homosexuals. Homosexuals are not bad people, just deceived sinners who need to repent of their sin.

The blood of Jesus Christ can wash away the sin of homosexuality just like any other sin:

"The blood of Jesus Christ his (God's) Son cleanseth us from *all* sin."   1 John 1:7

If you are a homosexual, you need Christ in your life. If you will receive Him as your personal Savior, He can set you free of this sin's demonic grasp.

A former homosexual who was wasting away in a hospital bed dying of AIDS said the following words to show how much having Jesus in his life means to him:

"I would rather have AIDS and have the relationship that I have with Jesus Christ than not have AIDS and not know Jesus Christ at all."[19]

God saved him, forgave him, and has since taken him to heaven. Because he received Jesus and repented of his sin, he will spend eternity with the Lord in paradise.

SEAN'S STORY

AIDS also claimed the life of Sean. But before he died, Sean told his story:

> "One day I spotted a man who was obviously gay and he was flirting as hard as he could and I was very flattered and I picked him up and drove over to his house and met a whole bunch of other guys and they all liked me, at least I thought they liked me.
>
> Obviously they wanted me for other reasons. That's when I first started getting caught up in the homosexual lifestyle.
>
> All the while it was like I was filling a round hole with a square peg... so I got very promiscuous. I would go to bookstores, bath houses, I would meet guys at bars and go home with them.
>
> I eventually got into prostitution and hustling because I was so unhappy I figured I might as well be making money off of this. It was all becoming

an act for me and the drugs helped me to go through the whole act and do all that kind of stuff.

The final moment came one afternoon when I was reading the New Testament and I was caught up with tears of joy. All of a sudden I just knew that Christ was the answer to fill the holes in my life.

I knew then that the way I had been living wasn't going to fulfill my needs. It wasn't right before God and it wasn't right for me. And I wanted to change."[20]

Within months of giving this interview, Sean died. But since he had received Jesus Christ as his Savior, he too is now enjoying the beauty of heaven!

THE TRUTH

Homosexuality is one more tool Satan is using to destroy millions of young lives and doom millions of souls to an eternity in hell. That's what every sin is designed to do.

But God loves homosexuals and wants to deliver them. That's why He sent His Son, Jesus, to die on the cross. God wants all people to repent of their sins and receive the gift of eternal life:

"The Lord is... not willing that *any*

(including homosexuals) should perish, but that all should come to repentance." 2 Peter 3:9

Please understand that homosexuals want you to keep having sex because it serves their interests. If you get AIDS and die, that's a sacrifice they are willing to make to continue in their sin. Don't let them make you a victim.

If you claim to be a homosexual Christian, but you still believe that God approves of homosexuality, you are living in powerful deception. God's infallible Word declares that He doesn't approve of it at all.

If you truly receive Jesus Christ into your life, He will show you that homosexuality is a wicked sin that needs to be repented of and forsaken.

If someone told you they were a Christian mass murderer and that God approved of their behavior because He made them that way, you would not believe it for a second.

The same is true of homosexuality. God hates it because He tells us so in His Word. Don't let the homosexual community's agenda cost you your life. Don't fall for their "safe sex" lies. Remain pure and live.

14

The Secret About Drugs

NOTICE: YOU HAVE WON the grand prize of TWO MILLION DOLLARS!

Jason's eyes almost popped out of his head when he saw those words on a registered letter he'd just pulled out of his mailbox. His hands began shaking as he looked at the letter.

It was true! He had really won. All he had to do was call a number and get the details on claiming his prize.

He rushed to the phone and called. A pleasant lady on the other end confirmed that he had in fact won TWO MILLION DOLLARS. All he had to do was come in and pick it up.

Jason couldn't wait! He laid awake at night dreaming of how he would spend the money. Streams of thoughts flowed through his head... cars—houses—trips—clothes...

The next day, Jason showed up 15 minutes early. A well-dressed woman greeted him and asked for identification. She congratulated him and told him to walk through the red curtain behind her to collect his check.

Jason's heart raced with excitement as he rushed around her desk. He was almost there. What happened next is a blur he will never forget.

SURPRISE!

As Jason stepped through the curtain, two police officers were waiting just inside. Each one grabbed an arm and faster than Jason could say "busted," he was handcuffed. A third officer appeared in front of him and read him his rights.

Then it hit him. You see, Jason was wanted for murder and armed robbery, but the police could never catch him. He always managed to stay one step ahead of them, so they tried a different approach. They enticed him with the promise of free money.

But instead of collecting his grand prize, Jason will spend the rest of his life behind bars in a state penitentiary.

SATAN'S SETUP

That's exactly how Satan uses drugs. Are drugs enticing? Of course. If they weren't, they wouldn't fulfill Satan's plan. If the devil told people in advance the damage that drugs would do to them, no one would ever start using them.

It would be like the police sending a letter to Jason saying:

> "Dear Jason, we want to arrest you for murder and armed robbery and send you up the river for the rest of your life. Please come down to the police station and turn yourself in. Thank you."
> Sincerely, the Police Department

Obviously, that would never work. The police had to be deceitful to lure their victim in. So they promised him two million dollars to entice him. Of course, they never had any intention of delivering. It was all a setup.

Through drugs, Satan promises euphoric highs and sublime peace, but all along, drugs are a tool the devil uses to fulfill his step by step plan for your destruction. Here's how it works:

ENTICEMENT

You don't need to be told how enticing drugs are. More than likely, you feel their pull every day. It's a powerful satanic pull that, in your own strength, can be very difficult to resist, even for Christian teens.

Plus, the devil is using every angle he can to heap the pressure on you. He'll whisper into your mind thoughts like:

- **"You won't be cool if you don't use them."**
- **"You're the only one in this school who isn't using them."**
- **"What are you, a goody-two-shoes?"**

If you are saying, "I only smoke pot, so I'll never have to worry about this," then the devil already has you well on the way to destruction.

Every teenager I've ever worked with who started taking heavy drugs began with pot. Many of them vowed they would *never* do anything stronger than pot, but they almost always did.

If you give in to the pressure and start taking drugs (including pot), the next step is:

INVOLVEMENT

For awhile, you may think you've found what you were looking for. The drugs may even deliver what they promised. The high may be great and all your worries and cares might be forgotten.

But each time you use drugs, you are inching a little closer to becoming a slave to them.

ALTERED STATE OF MIND

As you continue to use drugs, little by little your state of mind is changing. You can tell that it's happening by the new and different types of people you hang around with.

You probably don't even recognize it, but your thinking begins to get cloudy and your brain doesn't work quite the way it used to.

Many teens say they feel wiser and smarter when they're high, but that's just a lie from the devil to keep them from getting worried. In reality, all their thinking and reasoning abilities are being reduced.

CONTROL

This is where drug use becomes especially dangerous. Once your mind has become altered enough, it will reach a passive state that will allow demons to enter your soul and take over control of your life.

Once this happens, the demons begin driving you and you have less and less power to resist them.

If you've ever wondered why people do bizarre and destructive things while high on drugs that they normally would never do, it's because they are no longer in control of what they are doing. Now it's the demons in them who are calling the shots.

In my first book, *Stairway To Hell*, I describe

what happened to a young man named Steve.
When he was 18, Steve had a very frightening
experience. Here's part of what he said:

> "During a horrible experience with
> LSD, I had a shocking introduction
> to the spiritual realities of life. The
> devil was inside of me and quite
> systematically taking over control
> of my will.
>
> As I resisted the ever increasing
> pressure within me to take my
> control away... a voice inside of me
> kept saying, 'This time I will have
> you fully!' I was completely terrified!
> Somehow I knew that this was
> Satan..."[1]

How many times have you heard about
someone who murdered people or even killed
themself while high on drugs. That's because
the demons inside them wanted those people
dead. The person doing the killing is just a
vehicle the demons use to do their dirty work.

I'm convinced that our jails are full of people
who were driven by demons to commit
gruesome acts of murder that they'd never do
if demonic forces weren't controlling them.

Convicted mass murderer Jeffrey Dahmer
recently admitted on a television interview
that he was glad that he got caught and
was put in jail. He knew that it was the only

way to stop him from killing young boys. He said that he desperately wanted to stop, but couldn't.

BONDAGE

At this point, instead of the drugs serving you, you serve both the drugs and the demons behind them. The drugs you once loved have now brought you into bondage to a cruel master... Satan himself.

Now you **need** the drugs instead of wanting the drugs. Your life now revolves around drugs and you will do anything to get them.

At this point, marriages and families have broken up over drugs. Successful business people have lost entire careers over drugs. Others have stolen and even killed for drugs.

HARDEN YOUR HEART

One of the first things Satan will do once he controls you is harden your heart against God.

Satan hates God and will do **anything** to stop you from loving Him. If you are a Christian, his goal is to turn your heart away from God so you will give Satan (self) your worship.

If you are not yet a Christian, his goal is to make your heart so hard that you will never ask Jesus into your heart. He knows that if he can keep you away from Jesus, you will go to the lake of fire with him.

If you have ever tried to talk to someone about the Lord while they are high on drugs, you already understand this. It is impossible! The demons behind those drugs will never allow the person to listen. God warned us in His Word about how sin could harden our heart:

> "But exhort one another daily, while it is called To day; lest any of **you be hardened through the deceitfulness of sin.**"
>
> Hebrews 3:13

TORTURE

Remember John Lennon's quote a little earlier. This deceived musician was steeped in drugs and his remark to the preacher in his letter was, *"I want out of hell."*

In his suicide note, Kurt Cobain...

> "alluded to the chronic, undiagnosed pains in his 'burning, nauseous' stomach that had haunted him for years and had often made him consider suicide before."[2]

Interestingly, Cobain said heroin was the only thing that would stop the pain in his stomach.[3] That's just like Satan. The only way he could stop the pain was by taking something that would bring even more pain in the future. Young Kurt took each step, never knowing he was headed for his destruction.

It should make you hate the devil with a passion after seeing what he did to this young man. But it's nothing new. Satan has been torturing and killing young people for a long time. Sad to say, he's very good at it. But if you know what he's up to, you can stop him from getting you.

DEATH AND DESTRUCTION

This is Satan's ultimate goal for everyone. Satan is well aware that in the end, sin *always* kills:

> *"For the wages of sin is death;* but the gift of God is eternal life through Jesus Christ our Lord."
>
> Romans 6:23

He also knows that he can use sin to deceive people to bring about their death:

> "For sin, taking occasion by the commandment, *deceived me, and by it slew me."* Romans 7:11

If you are not yet a Christian, the lyrics to the song "Sacrifice" by Venom pretty well sum up the devil's desires for you:

> "Sacrifice/ Oh so nice/ Satan claims your soul/ Hail satanus/ Sacrifice to Lucifer my master/ Plunge the dagger in her breast/ I insist/ Demons rejoice/ Life is nothing to my lord..."

In fact, much of todays Heavy Metal music is very open and honest about what Satan wants for you. Check out how many songs and albums talk about death and hell. Here are just a few examples. There are hundreds more:

"Death Wish" — Metal Church

"Leave Me In Hell" — Venom

"Hell Patrol" — Raven

"Soul Destruction" — The Almighty

"Death Is Your Salvation" — Kreator

"See You In Hell" — Grim Reaper

"Make Them Die Slowly" — White Zombie

"Creeping Death" — Metallica

If you have never asked Jesus Christ to come into your heart, Satan has every available demon working overtime to make sure you don't. Hopefully, you won't let him win.

CHRISTIAN TEENS AND DRUGS

If you are a Christian, then you are Satan's arch enemy. He would kill you in a second if God allowed it.

And if you begin delving into drugs, even smoking pot, you are giving the devil legal ground in your life. That gives him the right to come into your life and begin his evil work.

Christian teen, please don't open that door.

Recognize drugs for what they are and avoid them.

KURT COBAIN AND RIVER PHOENIX

Kurt Cobain and River Phoenix are just two young men who took these steps and died, never knowing that the devil was carrying out their eternal death sentences.

Don't add your name to the list. Open your eyes now and realize that drugs are not something that happened to come along to make people feel good. They are a satanic tool that your enemy is using to carry out the execution of millions of people.

Please don't let him use this tactic on you.

15

The Secret About Abortion

Pat was 19. She and her boyfriend, Jim, were attending a Christian college when she became pregnant.

Jim's solution was simple... abortion!

After all, if they married, they would both lose the grants they were receiving to attend college. Plus, neither of them had time for a baby at that stage of their life.

But Pat hated even the thought of having an abortion. Night after night, she cried until she felt her heart would burst. Finally, she got down beside her bed and cried out to God and tried to explain why she was planning to go through with it.

When Pat arrived at the abortion clinic, she was taken into a procedure room. When a machine came on that sounded like a huge vacuum cleaner, Pat says:

> "From somewhere deep inside, my confusion, hurt and sorrow surfaced, and I began to cry. Rivers of tears welled out of my eyes... I must have been hysterical. The nurse turned off the machine and said she would get the doctor.

> "The next thing I knew, a white-coated man was standing beside me. 'I think you're going to keep your baby,' he told me... 'You want it far too much for me to ever perform this procedure.'"[1]

The doctor was right. Pat and Jim decided to keep the baby, get married and start their family. Today, their daughter is 8-years-old. Pat says:

> "When I look at my daughter... I can't imagine life without her."[2]

Pat was very fortunate. Her baby's life was spared and she avoided making one of the biggest mistakes of her life. But unfortunately, most pregnant girls who visit abortion clinics aren't as lucky.

FOR GIRLS ONLY

Teenage girl, I will speak mostly to you in this chapter because if you ever get pregnant and are forced to decide on this issue, it will be *you* who has the most at stake.

Many times, a boyfriend will try to pressure his pregnant girlfriend to have an abortion simply because that is the most convenient solution *for him*. And many other guys just disappear when they discover their girlfriend is pregnant.

In any case, teenage girl, you need to know the secret about abortion now—before someone tries to talk you into having one because that's what's best for them.

STAGGERING NUMBERS

Abortion is a hotly debated issue, but one fact is clear—millions of babies are dying:

> "More than one and one-half million American babies are killed each year through abortion."[3]

That means that in America alone, 177 babies are murdered every hour, 352 days a year.

Nearly 30 million unborn babies have been slaughtered in America.[4]

WHAT ABORTION IS PRESENTED AS

Medical "experts" claim that abortion is nothing more than the simple removal of some pregnancy tissue. Woman's groups contend that it's merely a question of a woman's right to choose.

But you are about to learn that there is far more to the abortion issue than what you are probably hearing.

THEY'LL NEVER TELL YOU THIS!

Thanks to ultrasound movies, doctors can now see the earliest development of babies. They can actually hear their little hearts beating only three or four weeks after conception.[5] That's usually before the mother even knows she's pregnant.

Tragically, no one in the abortion industry will ever tell you that your tiny baby has a heartbeat. Why? Because if there is a heartbeat, then the baby is obviously alive. And if the baby is alive, then having an abortion would obviously mean killing a living human being.

There are many other facts that abortionists will never tell you, like:

- By the 30th day, almost every one of the baby's organs has started to form.

- He can move his arms and legs by six weeks.

- By 43 days his brain waves can be read.

- By eight weeks, the baby has his very own fingerprints and *can feel pain.*

Abortionists are well aware that not many young ladies would knowingly kill their own baby. So, to keep the paying customers coming in, they keep their mouths shut.

Dr. John Wilke, an expert on the issue, reveals that abortionists tell young girls that:

> "This is only pregnancy tissue, my dear, just a glob—not really human yet, and all we're going to do is gently scrape out the products of pregnancy. They lie to them."[6]

ABORTION: THE GRAPHIC DETAILS

Few outside the abortion industry know the specifics involved in taking an unborn human's life. Once you read the following description of one type of abortion, you will know why they want to keep it quiet.

On September 13, 1993, the National Abortion Federation held a Risk Management Seminar which included a presentation by abortionist Dr. Martin Haskell entitled "Dilation and Extraction for Late Second Trimester Abortion."[7] In the presentation, Haskell graphically described the D & X abortion technique.

"The initial step in performing a D & X involves two days of dilating the mother's cervix. Afterward, the abortionist uses an ultrasound probe to locate the lower extremities of the unborn baby. He then works large grasping forceps through the mother's vaginal and cervical canals and into her uterus.

"The abortionist grasps a leg of the infant with the forceps and pulls the leg into the mother's vagina. The surgeon uses his fingers to deliver the opposite lower extremity, then the torso, the shoulders and the upper extremities. The skull lodges at the internal cervical os,"[8] Haskell explained.

"While clutching the baby's shoulders, the abortionist then 'takes a pair of blunt curved Metzenbaum scissors... He carefully advances the tip, curved down, along the spine and under his middle finger...

"The surgeon then forces the scissors into the base of the skull... Having safely entered the skull, he spreads the scissors to enlarge the opening. The surgeon removes the scissors and introduces a suction catheter into this hole and evacuates the skull contents. With the catheter still in place, he applies traction to the fetus, removing it completely from the patient."[9]

IN CASE YOU DIDN'T UNDERSTAND

In simple language, here's what the abortionist does. First, he delivers the entire baby except the head, which he leaves inside the mother, so it is not legally born.

Then he drives an instrument into the baby's head to make a hole. He enlarges the hole and sticks a vacuum cleaner through the hole into the baby's head and sucks out the unborn infant's brains and everything else in his or her head.

Once the baby is dead, the abortionist can remove the body from the mother without fear of prosecution. That's because our government has declared that if an abortionist kills a baby before it is delivered, he has done nothing illegal.

OTHER ABORTION TECHNIQUES

There are several other equally disgusting techniques used to abort little babies. Here is a brief description of a few:

• Dilation and Curettage (D & C):

A sharp scraping instrument is inserted into the uterus. The fetus is then cut into pieces and scraped from the uterine wall. A nurse must then reassemble the parts to make sure the uterus is empty.

• Suction Curettage (Vacuum Aspiration):

A tube is inserted into the uterus and connected to a strong suction apparatus. The vacuum is so powerful that the baby is torn to bits and sucked into a jar.

• Salt Poisoning (Saline Injection):

A long needle is used to inject a strong salt solution into the baby's sac. The baby swallows this poison and is literally burned alive. His outer layer of skin is completely burned off.

AN ABORTIONIST'S WORST NIGHTMARE

If you've ever heard that abortion isn't murder, you'll be interested to know why the D & X technique was invented in the first place.

It seems that one of the old methods, D & E (Dilation and Evacuation), was not effective enough. Too many babies were surviving abortions. Therefore, the abortionists needed a procedure with a higher death rate. Hence, the D & X technique.

Teenage girl, if that is just a glob or some pregnancy tissue inside of you, why are they so concerned about killing it before it's born?

Don't be deceived by their lies. If you are pregnant, that is a real live baby growing inside of you.

OTHER DANGERS OF ABORTION

Abortionists like to claim that their procedures are safe and simple. The truth is, they are neither. Statistics show that after a legal abortion, women face increased possibilities of future miscarriages, tubal pregnancies, premature births, sterility, and severe and long-lasting emotional disturbances.[10]

ONE STEP FURTHER— UNBORN BABY PARTS

It may seem unimaginable, but America has moved beyond simply butchering unborn babies and throwing them away. Now we have declared it legal to slice them up while they are still inside the womb and pull out body parts to be used for research and who knows what else.

On June 10, 1993, President Clinton signed into law the National Institutes of Health Revitalization Act of 1993. Part Two of this legislation authorized government funded research using tissue from aborted fetuses.[11]

To remove this tissue from unborn babies, doctors perform the D & X procedure we just discussed. However, in this case, after they cut open the back of the skull and suck out the brain material, if kidneys or other organs are desired, they are removed while the child is still partially in the vagina.[12]

The D & X technique is "perfect" for this because a baby born dead is of less value to researchers because brain tissue and other organs quickly deteriorate when deprived of oxygen.

Thus, the abortionist must find a way to remove the body parts and brain matter from a living baby who is not yet expelled from the birth canal.

A LIVE BABY IS A COMPLICATION

It's also important to remember that a child born alive is the ultimate "complication" to an abortionist because legally, every effort must be made to keep a breathing newborn alive. That's why the physician usually crushes the fetus' head while he or she is still in the uterus.

So for a baby to be most "valuable," it must be killed as close to delivery as possible, but not after delivery because the abortionist would then be forced to try and save the baby's life.

Isn't it interesting that when they want to make money from abortions, they say it's just a blob or some tissue inside. But at the same time they are devising new methods to legally harvest body parts from these unborn infants.

WHICH IS IT... A BLOB OR A BABY?

They can't have it both ways. Either it's a blob or it's a person. The truth is, the abortionists know it's a person. There is no denying the medical facts. With advanced technology like ultrasound movies, it has been proven conclusively that abortion is murder.

The abortionists know it's murder... they just don't want you to discover that fact. A former abortionist made this statement about his profession:

> "We just have to face it. Somebody has to do it. And unfortunately, we are the executioners..."[13]

GOD KNEW US BEFORE WE WERE BORN

Not only is a baby alive from the moment of conception, but God knew us all while we were still being formed in our mother's womb. God told Jeremiah the prophet:

> "Before I formed thee in the belly *I knew thee;* and before thou camest forth out of the womb I sanctified thee, and I ordained thee a prophet unto the nations."   Jeremiah 1:5

While Jeremiah was still inside his mother's womb, God set him apart and ordained him as a prophet. Thank God his life wasn't aborted. The Psalmist King David said:

> "For thou hast possessed my reins: *thou hast covered me in my mother's womb."*   Psalm 139:13

Throughout the Bible, it's made clear that the little lives growing inside of their mother's wombs are little human beings.

GOD HATES THE KILLING OF BABIES

God sends a strong message to those who murder innocent babies:

> "These six things doth the Lord hate... *hands that shed innocent blood."*   Proverbs 6:16,17

One of God's Ten Commandments confirms how God feels about killing others:

> "And God spake all these words, saying... *Thou shalt not kill."*
>   Exodus 20:1,13

THE REAL ENEMY

It is crucial that you understand one point. The real enemy in all this is not the doctors, the abortion clinic workers or the women's rights advocates. And it's not the people who march up and down the streets promoting a woman's right to choose.

These people are just pawns doing Satan's dirty work. They are not necessarily bad people, they have simply been deceived by the master deceiver—Satan. When God casts Satan into the bottomless pit, it will be to stop him from deceiving people:

> "And cast him (Satan) into the bottomless pit, and shut him up, and set a seal upon him, *that he should deceive the nations no more..."*   Revelation 20:3

Sometimes even Christians think those who perform abortions are the enemy, but they're not. They are certainly involved in a wicked work and will pay a terrible price for this sin when they stand before God, but they are not the enemy. The real enemy is Satan himself.

Christians should earnestly pray that God would open the eyes of those who promote or perform abortions and show them that Satan is using them to do his killing for him.

Satan doesn't care that these people will suffer horrible judgment for the deeds they are performing, any more than he cares about the innocent babies they are murdering.

For centuries, the devil has been using people to murder babies. That's because he has always been a murderer:

> "Ye are of your father the devil, and the lusts of your father ye will do. *He was a murderer from the beginning...*" John 8:44

CHILD MURDER IS NOTHING NEW

History is filled with cultures that sacrificed their children to false gods (Satan). In Old Testament times, Queen Jezebel led the Israelites in Baal (Satan) worship and the sacrifice of children. The children were placed on large circular altars, then were rolled into a blazing fire.[14]

The Greek author Kleitarchos describes the practice of sacrificing infants 300 years before Christ:

> "Out of reverence for Kronos (Baal), the Phoenicians... whenever they seek to obtain some great favor, vow one of their children, ***burning it as a sacrifice to the deity (Satan)...***"[15]

Down through the ages, many cultures have sacrificed infants to pagan gods. Whether the people knew it or not, they were sacrificing their children to Satan. The only difference today is that we kill them before removing them from the womb, instead of after.

THERE IS FORGIVENESS

Teenage girl, if you have already had an abortion and now struggle with the fact that you murdered your baby, you need to know that God's forgiveness is available.

First, you must understand that any sin, including abortion, can be forgiven. If you will receive Jesus Christ as your personal Savior, you can have *all* your sins forgiven:

> "Therefore if any man be in Christ, he is a new creature: old things are passed away; behold, ***all things are become new.***" 2 Corinthians 5:17

Then, once you have been born into God's

family, He will forgive any sin you commit if you will confess it to Him:

> "If we confess our sins, he is faithful and just to forgive us our sins, and to cleanse us from **all unrighteousness.**"   1 John 1:9

The best part is, once you ask God to forgive your sins, He not only forgives them but he also **forgets** them. God Himself says:

> "I, even I, am he that blotteth out thy transgressions for mine own sake, and **will not remember thy sins.**"   Isaiah 43:25

If God has forgiven and forgotten your sin, you need to forgive yourself and let go of it. If you believe that God could never forgive you, or that this sin is too awful to be forgiven, then you are listening to lies that Satan is planting in your mind.

God says you **can** be forgiven... the devil says you **can't.** Please don't let the devil keep you in bondage any longer by believing his lies.

Believe the truth. God loves you and wants to forgive you for what you've done. He wants to heal you and fill your heart with peace. Please let him do it right now.

If you have never had an abortion, please don't be deceived by the lies of the pro-abortion crowd. They care about what's best for them, not what's best for you. Before you agree to have an abortion, please understand that abortion is the cold-blooded murder of a helpless unborn baby.

Please don't ever do it.

16

The Secret About Violence Among Teens

"CHARLES CONRAD DIDN'T HAVE A CHANCE. He was 55 years old, crippled by multiple sclerosis and needed a walker or wheelchair to get around.

The boys who allegedly attacked him were young—17, 15 and 14— and they were ruthless.

Police say that when Conrad returned to his suburban Atlanta condominium while they were burgling it, the boys got rid of him. Permanently.

Over a period of many hours... they stabbed him with a kitchen knife and a barbecue fork, strangled him with a rope, and hit him on the head with a hammer and the barrel of a shotgun, according to a statement one of the boys... reportedly gave to the police.

Despite this torture, Conrad survived. According to the statement published by *The Atlanta Journal-Constitution*, a grievously wounded Conrad begged the boys to shoot him and put a swift end to his agony. But... the boys were afraid people would hear the gunshots.

So they allegedly beat him some more, and then poured salt into his wounds to see if he was still alive. When his body twitched in response to the pain, they threw household knickknacks at him. After he was struck in the back by a brass eagle, 'he stopped breathing.'

The boys then took off in Conrad's wheelchair-equipped van with their hard-earned loot: a stereo, a VCR, a camcorder and a shotgun..."[1]

There is no question that we live in a violent society. And in a large number of instances, teenagers are either the victims of violent acts or the ones committing them.

Unbelievably, stories like this are becoming commonplace. A growing number of teens literally fear for their lives every day. Many wonder where all this violence is coming from.

> "According to the FBI, more than 2,200 murder victims in 1991 were under 18—an average of more than six young people killed every day."[2]

> "The Justice Department estimates that each year, nearly a million young people between 12 and 19 are raped, robbed or assaulted, often by their peers."[3]

That's almost 3,000 of these types of crimes every day of the year.

> "More than three million crimes a year are committed in or around America's 85,000 public schools."[4]

MURDER IN A SCHOOL HALLWAY

In January, 1993, in the hallway of Norland Senior High School in Miami, Florida, several boys started arguing over a girl.

Words were exchanged, and the situation quickly became heated. When one young man pulled a pistol, so did 18-year-old senior Conroy Robinson. What followed was a literal shootout in the crowded school hallway.

At least three guns were blazing when teachers finally arrived on the scene. When calm was restored, Robinson was found laying dead in a pool of blood, with more than a dozen bullet holes in his body.[5]

> "Murder is the second-leading cause of death among teens, after auto accidents. It accounts for more teen deaths than all natural causes combined."

> "Every day, an estimated 270,000 guns go to school with students."[7]

WHY IS IT SO VIOLENT?

A big part of the reason that teens are facing so much violence is that they are saying "no" to God. Sadly, even many Christian teens refuse to obey His clear commands.

When we repeatedly rebel against the Lord, we forfeit His divine protection and blessings.

> "For rebellion is as the sin of witchcraft, and stubbornness is as iniquity and idolatry. Because thou hast rejected the word of the LORD, he hath also rejected thee..."
>
> 1 Samuel 15:23

For example, look what's happened to public schools since we kicked God out. When God left, Satan gladly strolled in and took over. Now we're paying the price:

"In the 1940's, the main problems students faced were talking and chewing gum in class. Today, their problems include drugs, rape, robbery and assault."[8]

Secondly, teens, both Christian and non-Christian, are not only saying "no" to God, but they are willingly saying "yes" to the devil.

When you choose to do the devil's bidding, you open doorways, giving Satan and his demons legal ground to bring destruction into your life.

"The way of the Lord is strength to the upright: *but destruction shall be to the workers of iniquity.*"
Proverbs 10:29

"It is a joy to the just to do judgment: *but destruction shall be to the workers of iniquity.*"
Proverbs 21:15

The more you open doorways, the more control you give Satan in your life. And the more control you give him, the more he can use you to do his evil deeds.

Behind most violent acts are demons, who, behind the scenes, are urging the turmoil and confusion on. Usually, the young people involved have no idea what is happening in the spiritual world.

Whenever you hear about a violent crime, realize that hidden in the shadows, Satan and his demons are driving the young people to do their dirty work.

Look at the story at the beginning of this chapter. Do you really believe that a group of teenage boys could be such heartless, cold-blooded murderers on their own? No! Their violent actions were totally fueled by demonic forces.

SATAN'S TOOLS

Here are a few of the devil's favorite and most effective tools for creating violence and destruction:

• DRUGS:

We've already discussed drugs, so we won't repeat it here. But how many people have you heard about who have committed violent acts like murder, rape and suicide while high on drugs?

When you take drugs, you are connecting with demons—very violent demons.

• ALCOHOL:

Alcohol is also being widely used by Satan to bring about untold violence. More often than not, he uses teens to carry out his dirty deeds.

DRUNK TEENS MURDER MENTALLY RETARDED MAN

Two boys, Herman Snell, 14, and Johnny Jumper, 17, both from Salina, Oklahoma are charged with first-degree murder for the brutal slaying of Robert Ballard, a 33-year-old mentally retarded man.

Townspeople were furious when a newspaper photo showed the two boys smiling as they were being led to the Mayes County courtroom for their preliminary hearing.

Then, in court, as everyone else cried, the two boys snickered when the medical examiner testified that chunks from a computer toy were found embedded in Ballard's skull.

> "Snell joked that after the beating that Ballard's eyeball was missing and he could poke his finger through the socket."[9]

The boys admitted drinking beer and a mixture of 190-proof alcohol prior to the attack. When an investigator asked Snell why he beat Ballard, he responded, **"I was drunk."**[10]

Snell's mother said of the hideous murder:

> "Neither one of them would have done something like this in their right mind."[11]

• **ROCK MUSIC:**

Following is the true story of Laurie Lynne Rakowski as it was told to Alan and Jo Anne Woody:

> "Mommy and I had such a loving relationship that some of my

friends remarked about how close we were. I enjoyed being with her so much that I would often rush home after school so she and I could spend time together before the rest of the family came home.

When I was 13 years old I was invited to go to a rock music concert... Mommy did not know all the kids... but I begged to go and she slowly agreed. I was so excited!

We arrived early and got some seats near the front. As the music got louder and louder and the crowd got wilder and wilder, I looked over at my friends and their fresh faces had lost all traces of love and laughter.

I wanted to run out of that place as fast as I could, but I was nearly covered with sweating, screaming bodies trying to drown out the shrieking, ear-splitting sound coming from the stage.

I tried to break away but they began to pull at my hair and tear my clothes. I screamed for them to stop but it did no good. They seemed to be in a trance.

About two months later I was invited

to (another) one but I screamed 'No! No! No!' I was told that it would be much milder than the other one. When it came time to go to the concert I was ready.

It did seem more civilized than the first one, or perhaps it was just as bad and I was becoming less civilized. Anyhow, before long I was hung up on that music and I listened to it day and night. In a short period of time I was hooked.

Before I knew it my interests, attitude and actions began to change. I became extremely moody and depressed. I became quick tempered and threatening.

I also started taking (prescription drugs), but I went on into the harder stuff, like cocaine and crack. The arguments with my parents got worse and our once happy home began to fall apart.

One evening Mommy tried to keep me from leaving the house to meet some of my friends and I threw a temper tantrum and got a gun and shot her. She fell on the floor and looked up at me with an expression I shall never, never forget.

> When I realized what I had done
> I got down on the floor and cried,
> 'Mommy, Mommy! Please don't die!
> Please don't leave me! Please give
> me another chance!'"

Before help arrived, Laurie's precious mother and dearest friend was dead."[12]

Can't you see what happened to Laurie? Obviously, she didn't want her mother dead, or she would never have cried out: "Mommy! Please don't die! Please don't leave me!"

The demons behind the rock music that took control of her life are the ones who wanted to see blood flow. And once the rock music brought Laurie under Satan's control, he used her to commit the murder for him.

TEEN KILLS POLICEMAN

For many years, rock music has been wide open about it's desire to cause death. A well known rock group sings a song called *"Murder by the Numbers:"*

> **"Murder is like anything else -- you take to.**
> **It's a habit-forming need for more and more.**
> **You can bump off every member of your family**
> **or anyone else you find a bore."**

Ronald, a 19-year-old from Texas, was charged

with the murder of a Texas Highway Trooper. According to accounts, Howard was driving a stolen car and listening to a tape of rapper Tupac Amuru Shakur's violence-laced "2PACALYPSENOW." The album includes six songs that portray the killing of police officers.

Howard told authorities that he was listening to "2PACALYPSENOW" as he loaded his weapon, aimed it at the officer and pulled the trigger. [13]

Other rock groups sing about killing children just to hear them scream. And several songs encourage suicide as a good way to end your problems.

Even if you don't listen to those groups or those songs, the same devil is behind the rock music that you do listen to. And when you say "no" to God and "yes" to Satan in the area of music, you open yourself up for the same kind of attack... and the same results, no matter how good a Christian you may feel you are.

Satan's desires for you are the same as his desires for Laurie and her mother. At one point Laurie never wanted to do anything that would upset her mother. But when Satan was finished with her, she murdered her mother in cold blood.

• **SUICIDE:**

Every teen I've ever talked to who tried to commit suicide had one thing in common. At some point in their attempt, they realized they didn't really want to die and began struggling to save their life. That's because it wasn't them who wanted to die, it was the demons that controlled them who wanted them dead.

• THE OCCULT:

Again, we have already covered the violence associated with satanism and the occult, so we need not go over it again. But be careful. You probably won't run into someone carrying a big sign that says "I am a satanist and I want to destroy you."

Watch out for his subtle recruiting tactics like ouija boards, New Age gimmicks, astrology, false religions. All these can provide open doorways for demons to begin taking control of your life.

• GANGS:

Gang members don't know it, but they are being used by Satan in the worst way. First, they are out there on the front lines, doing Satan's killing and destroying for him. He's filled their heads with so many lies that they can't see him and his demons helping them aim the guns and pull the triggers.

And when the devil is done using them to send others to hell, he'll blow them away, leaving them to face an eternity in the lake of fire! These young people are laying their lives on the line for someone who wants them to burn in hell. They are being used by demonic spirits—and don't even know it.

> "Wherein in time past ye walked according to the course of this world, according to the prince of the power of the air (Satan), *the spirit that now worketh in the children of disobedience:*"
>
> Ephesians 2:2

• BRAINWASHING:

Look at our entertainment. Violence is everywhere—children's cartoons, television and movies. Satan is bombarding young people with a flood of violence:

> "By the time teenagers reach age 18, they have seen some 40,000 murders on T.V."[14]

Nikki Sixx of *Motley Crue* said the following about today's youth:

> "They're young, *they can be brainwashed and programmed.*"[15]

He's right! Many teens are being brainwashed and programmed... *for destruction!*

WHAT CAN WE DO ABOUT IT?

To protect yourself from violence, the only good choice is to get right with God, then find His will for your life and begin doing it. God takes great care of His children:

> "Because thou hast made the Lord,

which is my refuge, even the most High, thy habitation;

There shall no evil befall thee, neither shall any plague come nigh thy dwelling.

For he shall give his angels charge over thee, to keep thee in all thy ways.

They shall bear thee up in their hands, lest thou dash thy foot against a stone."   Psalm 91:9-12

NO NEED TO FEAR

In violent times like these, it's comforting to know that you have a heavenly Father who is watching over you and protecting you.

The world can be destroying itself all around you, but if you will follow and obey God, He will protect you from all danger.

Please, forsake the world and turn to Jesus. He wants to protect you. Will you let Him?

"The angel of the Lord encampeth round about them that fear him, and delivereth them."   Psalm 34:7

"When I cry unto thee, then shall mine enemies turn back: this I know; for God is for me."

Psalm 56:9

17

Satan's Favorite Word

Can you guess the devil's favorite word?

Here are two clues.

ONE: It leads more people to hell than anything else.

TWO: It destroys more teenagers than any other satanic tool.

Probably, words like "drugs," "alcohol," "immorality," etc. are popping into your head. Sorry, but none of these even come close to Satan's favorite word.

Satan's favorite word is... religion!

The devil loves religion! For centuries he has used religions to deceive billions of people and lead them into the flames of hell.

You need to understand that I am not talking about Christianity here, I'm talking about religion. The two are completely different.

Religion is people working at following a bunch of man-made rules in hopes of doing enough good works to earn their way into heaven. That's what most of the world has.

But true Christianity is people being born into God's family by receiving Jesus Christ as their Savior. Once they are part of God's family, they develop a personal relationship with Him. This is God's plan for us, according to His Holy Word.

A TICKET TO HEAVEN

There are two specific ways Satan is using religion to deceive and destroy young people.

First, many teens are counting on a religion to get them to heaven. They figure that obeying the rules of their religion will get them in. But that will NEVER happen. Performing good works has never saved anybody—and it never will. God's Word says:

> "Knowing that a man is not justified by the works of the law, but by the faith of Jesus Christ, even we

> have believed in Jesus Christ, that
> we might be justified by the faith
> of Christ, and not by the works of
> the law: for by the works of the law
> shall no flesh be justified."
>
> Galatians 2:16

Unfortunately, many young people who attend Bible believing, Bible preaching churches have nothing more than a religion, although the devil has deceived them into thinking they have a relationship with Christ.

Many teens have wondered why they had no joy or victory in their Christian life. Then they discovered that they only had a religion, not a relationship with Christ.

Once they were born again and began a real relationship with Jesus Christ, God started doing miraculous things in their life.

Many church youth groups are filled with members who think they have a relationship, but in truth, they have nothing more than a religion.

I urge you to examine your life. Ask God right now if you really have a personal relationship with Him, or if your faith is in the good works of a religion or a church.

If you are genuinely a born again Christian, this chapter is not designed to cause you to doubt your salvation. Instead, it's purpose is to open the eyes of teens who believe they are God's children when they really aren't.

Satan is a master deceiver. Don't let him deceive you on this one. Eternity in heaven or hell is at stake.

"NO THANKS, I'VE HAD ENOUGH!

Then there's the second well-oiled trick of the enemy. Many have fallen for it.

First, Satan convinces you that religion and Christianity are the same thing. Then he shows you the hypocrisy of religion, knowing you will get bitter and quit, wanting nothing more to do with religion of any sort.

This is where the devil will get you. Since you are assuming that Christianity and religion are the same, when you give up on religion, you'll also give up on Christianity at the same time.

What you need to know is that it's okay to give up on religion, just don't give up on Christ. All religions belong to Satan. God wants nothing to do with them. He wants you to be born into His family and have a relationship with His Son, Jesus.

When you go to a church, you need to find out what they teach. Do they want you to put your faith in the rules of their religion, or do they urge you to become a child of God through faith in the Lord Jesus Christ?

GARY'S STORY

For 20 years, Gary had a religion. He performed all the religious duties that were expected of him, but he had nothing inside his heart. And if he had died, he'd have gone straight to hell.

When a friend told Gary that he needed a personal relationship with Jesus Christ, his first words were:

> "No thanks. I've gone to church all my life and it was all phony."

Fortunately for Gary, his friend was persistent. Finally, Gary agreed to attend his church and see what it was like. During his first visit, Gary discovered what it meant to have a relationship with Jesus.

At the end of the service, a young man opened his Bible and introduced Gary to Jesus. Right then, Gary began a personal relationship with Jesus Christ. He also realized what a mistake he had made when he gave up on God because a religion had failed him.

Since then, Gary hasn't needed a religion—because he has Christ. And you don't need a religion either. You need Jesus in your life.

ALL RELIGIONS CAN'T BE RIGHT!

Look at the following verse of scripture:

> "Enter ye in at the strait gate: for wide is the gate, and broad is the

> way, that leadeth to destruction,
> **and many there be which go in
> thereat:**
>
> Because strait is the gate, and
> narrow is the way, which leadeth
> unto life, and *few* there be that find
> it."   Matthew 7:13-14

Think about that. Most people in the world
have a religion, yet God declaress that only a
few will go to heaven. How tragic that billions
of people hope to reach heaven by following
a religion, when all along God said a religion
won't get anyone in.

A married couple faithfully served as foreign
missionaries for their religion for 50 or 60
years, believing their lifetime of good works
and sacrifice would get them into heaven. But
God's Word already said that good works can
never buy anyone a ticket into heaven:

> "Many will say to me in that day,
> Lord, Lord, have we not prophesied
> in thy name? and in thy name have
> cast out devils? and in thy name
> done many wonderful works?
>
> And then will I profess unto them, *I
> never knew you: depart from me,*
> ye that work iniquity."
>   Matthew 7:22-23

Yes, young person, the unchanging truth is
that there is only *one* way to get to Heaven.

It's through faith in Jesus Christ. No religion can get you there. Religions are a tool of Satan to get people into hell's fires. Jesus said:

> "I am the way the truth and the life. No man cometh to the Father *but by me.*"   John 14:6

Jesus hates religions because he knows they lead people into eternal damnation. Look how he talked to the religious leaders of His day:

> "But woe unto you, scribes and Pharisees, hypocrites! for ye shut up the kingdom of heaven against men: *for ye neither go in yourselves,* neither suffer ye them that are entering to go in.
>
> Woe unto you, scribes and Pharisees, hypocrites! for ye devour widow's houses, and for a pretence make long prayer: therefore *ye shall receive the greater damnation...*
>
> Even so ye also outwardly appear righteous unto men, but within ye are *full of hypocrisy and iniquity...*
>
> Ye serpents, ye generation of vipers, *how can ye escape the damnation of hell."*   Matthew 23:13,14,28,33

If you are counting on a religion to get you to heaven, don't be deceived any longer. NO RELIGION will EVER get you there.

And if you have given up on Jesus because you were burned by a religion, don't let the devil use that bad experience to keep you away from Christ any longer. Avoid religions, but don't reject Christ:

- **Religion takes people to hell, but Christianity leads people to heaven:**

    "He that believeth on the Son hath everlasting life: and he that believeth not the Son shall not see life; but the wrath of God abideth on him."   John 3:36

- **Religions bring people into bondage. Christ sets people free!**

    "And ye shall know the truth, and the truth *shall make you free."*
                                   John 8:32

- **Religion keeps people in the dark, but Christianity leads people to the light. Jesus said:**

    "I am the light of the world: he that followeth me shall not walk in darkness, *but shall have the light of life."*   John 8:12

- **Religion takes, but Jesus gives.**

    "He that spared not his own Son, but delivered him up for us all, how shall he not with him also *freely give us all things?"*
                                   Romans 8:32

- **Religion stresses people out, Jesus gives people rest:**

    "Come unto me, all ye that labour and are heavy laden, and *I will give you rest.*"   Matthew 11:28

Which do you have right now? A religion or a relationship? If you haven't already done so, begin a relationship with Jesus right now. You'll be amazed at what God can do in your life.

You Might Be Blind and Not Even Know It

If you've read this whole book and still refuse to accept Jesus as your Savior, there's only one explanation.

YOU HAVE BEEN BLINDED!

No, not physically blinded, *spiritually* blinded.

That is Satan's ultimate con—first he blinds you so that you cannot see the truth, then he convinces you that it was *your* decision to reject Christ, not his:

> "In whom the god of this world (Satan) *hath blinded the minds of them which believe not* lest the

light of the glorious gospel of Christ, who is the image of God, should shine unto them."

2 Corinthians 4:4

Millions of teens have been blinded by the devil. They are rejecting Christ, but don't even know why.

You may not have decided for yourself to live a miserable existence, then die and go to hell. It might be that Satan, the deceiver, is making that decision for you.

You don't even have to believe God on this one. Satan's servants have been telling you the same thing for years. Listen to some lyrics from the Iron Maiden song, *"Can I Play With Madness:"*

> ***"You're too blind to see...***/I said, you'll pay for your mischief/In this world or the next/Oh then he fixed me with a freezing glance/And the hellfires raged in his eyes/And you wanna know the truth, son/Lord, I'll tell you the truth/Your soul's gonna burn in a Lake of Fire."

If you are a Christian, it may not have been your decision to turn your back on Christ and suffer the consequences of serving your flesh. Satan may have blinded your mind through the deceitfulness of sin.

My prayer is that before you finish reading this chapter, you will decide that you want to break off that satanic blindness and see the beautiful truths that can set you free and fill your life with peace and joy.

PETER'S STORY

Peter was saved at the age of 10, but by 14 he was overcome by the lusts of the world. He found a girlfriend who introduced him to drugs and rock music.

But Peter's mom prayed for her son every day. Each time she mentioned to Peter that he should be living for the Lord, Peter laughed, and told her that Christianity was for losers and old people.

But Peter's world gradually fell apart. He became a slave to the drugs he once loved. Rather than wanting them, he *needed* them and did anything necessary to get them. His girlfriend dumped him, and his parents eventually threw him out.

With no home, no food and no money, Peter's view of life changed dramatically. One cold, damp night while laying on a park bench, Peter recalled a previous conversation with his mother.

She had explained to him that Satan was using sin to blind his mind. She informed him that she prayed every night for God to bind the demons that were stopping him from seeing the truth.

"FINALLY, I CAN SEE!"

As Peter lay on that park bench, his mother's prayers were answered. Desperate for help, Peter quietly kneeled at the bench and bound, in Jesus' name, every demonic force that had blinded his mind.

He then prayed and asked God to forgive all of his sins and remove the spiritual blindness so he could know what he needed to do.

Within minutes Peter realized how deceived he had been. He rededicated his life to God and renewed his relationship with his Heavenly Father.

After he prayed, a sweet peace flooded Peter's body. Almost instantly, he realized that for all those years his mind had been blinded by the devil. The truth had been right there in front of him, but he wasn't able to see it.

But now it was so easy to see. He couldn't believe that he had been so blind. He raced home and excitedly shared the good new with his mother, and they both rejoiced together.

Peter had always been so sure that he knew what he was doing, but now he clearly understood verses like this one:

> "There is a way *which seemeth right unto a man;* but the end

thereof are the ways of death."

Proverbs 14:12

YOU DON'T HAVE TO STAY BLIND

Has the devil blinded your mind? If so, you don't have to stay blind another minute. Your spiritual eyesight can be restored. When the Apostle Paul was converted, God sent him to people:

> *"To open their eyes,* and to turn them from darkness to light, and from the power of Satan unto God, that they may receive forgiveness of sins, and inheritance among them which are sanctified by faith that is in me."   Acts 26:18

If you have never received Jesus Christ as your Savior, that's what God wants to do for you right now. He wants to turn you from darkness to light, from the power of Satan to the Almighty power of God.

My prayer for you right now is that every demon that is blinding your mind and stopping you from receiving Jesus as your Savior would be bound in Jesus' name.

If you can now see that you have been blinded and need Jesus in your life, please pray a prayer like this from your heart:

> Dear Lord Jesus, I accept you as my Savior. Please forgive my sins and

come into my heart and save me. In
Jesus' name, Amen.

If you prayed that prayer and really meant it,
God just removed the blindness and gave you
a brand new spiritual eyesight.

If you are already a Christian, but you know
the devil has blinded you through sin, please
pray a prayer like this in your own words:

Dear God,

Because of sin, Satan has blinded
my eyes and led me into sin. But
I don't want him deceiving me or
running my life any longer.

So, in the name of Jesus Christ, I
take authority over every deceiving
spirit that has stopped me from
seeing what God wants me to see
and in His name I bind all of you
from off of my life.

Father, I ask you to remove the
blindness and restore my spiritual
eyesight so I can fulfill Your will for
my life. In Jesus' name, Amen.

TANYA'S STORY

Tanya was born and raised in a Christian
home. She asked Jesus into her heart when
she was 9, but she saw so much hypocrisy at
church that when she became a teenager, she
had no desire to live the Christian life.

Each year her heart grew harder and she became more hateful towards every aspect of Christianity. Her parents tried to talk to her several times but her standard response was "I don't want to hear it,"

Other people tried to discuss the Lord with her, but she turned them down every time.

Each night Tanya's parents prayed that God would bind the demons that were blinding her from seeing the truth.

Finally, while laying in bed one night, Tanya began to "see." She prayed and asked God to forgive her for turning her back on Him. Then she bound Satan and his demons in Jesus' name and commanded them to stop blinding her:

> "Submit yourselves therefore to God. Resist the devil, **and he will flee from you."**   James 4:7

God was faithful and her relationship with Jesus Christ was restored. The demonic blindness was broken off. She now looks back and marvels:

> "I can't believe how blind I was. I was miserable, but I still rejected the truth. I really thought I knew what I was doing, but now I see that Satan had me totally deceived."

Has Satan blinded your mind, teen? Here's

how you can tell. If you have rejected Christ, why did you reject Him?

Was it because you carefully studied the scriptures and decided that you did not want what Christ had to offer? Or did you let the devil make the decision for you?

It's interesting that teenagers usually want to use their own judgment and make their own decisions. Yet when it comes to salvation, many blindly accept the untrue thoughts Satan puts into their minds, and reject Christ on the basis of those lying thoughts.

Please don't let the most important decision in your life be made by your worst enemy.

4 STEPS TO CLEAR SIGHT

If you would like to have the blindness lifted and be able to see spiritually, here are four steps you must take:

STEP ONE

The first step is to accept Jesus as your Savior. Without Him in your heart you are spiritually dead, and you don't stand a chance:

> "But the natural man *receiveth not the things of the Spirit of God: for they are foolishness unto him:* neither can he know them, because they are spiritually dis-cerned."   1 Corinthians 2:14

STEP TWO

The second step is to confess and forsake any sin in your life. Continually practicing sin gives Satan legal ground to come into your life and blind your mind. To see spiritually, the sin has got to go.

> "But exhort one another daily, while it is called To day; lest any of you be *hardened through the deceitfulness of sin.*" Hebrews 3:13

STEP THREE

The third step is to bind the enemy in Jesus' name. Demons must obey *anything* that is commanded in the name and authority of Jesus Christ.

When Jesus sent out 70 of His followers on a mission, they returned saying:

> "...Lord, even the devils are subject unto us *through thy name.*"
> Luke 10:17

If you bind any deceiving spirits in the name of Jesus Christ, they will not be allowed to blind your mind.

STEP FOUR

The fourth thing you must do is remove any idols from your life.

> "The idols of the heathen are silver and gold, the work of men's hands.

They have mouths, but they speak not; eyes they have, but they see not; They have ears, but they hear not...

They that make them are like unto them; so is every one that trusteth in them."

Psalm 135:15-18

Do you have any idols, young person? If anything in your life is more important to you than Jesus Christ, it's an idol. It could be a boyfriend, a girlfriend, your music, your friends, drugs... it can be anything!

If you have idols in your life, the devil will use them to render you as blind and deaf as a wooden statue sitting on a shelf.

To break that blindness off, you **MUST** dump your idols and elevate Jesus Christ to the number one position in your life.

ARE YOU BLIND, CHRISTIAN TEEN?

Many Christians teens have fallen into deception in this area, thinking they are immune to the devil's ability to blind their mind simply because they are a child of God.

They think they can live in sin and get away with it because they are a Christian. But when you, Christian or not, wallow in sin, you give Satan legal ground to move in and blind your mind and deceive you.

If you will confess your idol worship as sin and turn your back on the idols, God will forgive you.

Teen, God doesn't want you to be blind. He wants you to be free from demonic blindness so you can walk in truth and light. If you would like to be set free right now, pray a prayer like this one:

> Heavenly Father,
>
> I admit that I have sinned. I now confess every single sin and ask you to forgive me for each one (confess every sin you can think of).
>
> In Jesus' name I bind every demonic spirit that has blinded me in any way and I claim the power of your precious blood over them.
>
> Lord, please reveal your truth to me so I can be set free. In Jesus' name, Amen.

Don't let the devil keep you in spiritual darkness. Learn the truth and be set free:

> "And ye shall know the truth, and the truth shall make you free."
>
> John 8:32

God bless you as you put the truths you have learned in this book into practice.

Footnotes

Introduction
  1. *Baptist New Mexican*, Aug. 5, 1989, Pg. 3.

Chapter 1
  1. John Muncy, *The Role Of Rock*, Daring Pub. Group, Canton, Ohio, 1989, pg. 288.

Chapter 3
  1. *PEOPLE* magazine, April 25, 1994, pg. 40.
  2. *PEOPLE* magazine, Jan. 17, 1994, pg. 58.
  3. *TIME* magazine, Oct. 25, 1993, pg. 62.

Chapter 4
  1. *Baptist New Mexican*, August 5, 1989, pg. 3.
  2. *Baptist New Mexican*, June 2, 1990, pg. 1.
  3. *Scholastic Update*, Jan. 14, 1994, pg. 9.

4. *The New York Times*, June 9,1990, pg. 8.
5. *TEEN*, April, 1991, pg. 28.
6. Ibid., pg. 29.
7. *Science News*, Oct. 5, 1991, pg. 218.
8. Stewart Regan, *Michael Jackson*, Greenwich House, 1984, pg. 53.
9. David Sheff & G. Barry Golson, *The Playboy Interviews with John Lennon & Yoko Ono*, Berkley Books, New York, 1981, ppg. 202-203.
10. *TIME* magazine, Oct. 25, 1993, pg. 63.
11. Ibid., pg. 62.
12 *The Mediator*, Vol. 9, Issue 2, pg. 2.
13. *Bloomington Herald-Telephone*, Jan. 14, 1986.
14. Second Chance, *Raunch Rock Reaping Cruel Fruit*, 1989, Pg.7.
15. Ibid.

Chapter 5
1. *The Little Cloud Report*, June 1994, pg. 5.
2. *PEOPLE* magazine, April 18, 1994, pg. 34.
3. Daily News, September 14, 1988, pg. 11.
4. *Los Angeles Times*, May 25, 1994, pg. A-1.
5. *Womans World*, Feb. 6, 1990, ppg. 14-15.

Chapter 9
1. ASAP family Information sheet © 1986
2. Ibid.
3. Ibid.
4. *The Phyllis Schlafly Report*, Nov. 1990, pg. 2.
5. *U.S. New & World Report*, Apr. 18, 1994, pg. 43.
6. Ibid., pg. 34.
7. Ibid., pg. 38.
8. Ibid., pg. 35.
9. Ibid., pg. 35.
10. *U.S. New & World Report*, Apr. 18, 1994, pg. 38.

11. *USA TODAY,* June 22, 1994, pg. 1A.
12. *U.S. News & World Report,* Apr. 18, 1994, pg. 43.
13. *The Phyllis Schlafly Report,* Nov., 1990, pg. 2.
14. *FORTUNE,* November 4, 1991, pg. 173, 176.
15. Ibid., pg. 173.
16. Ibid., pg. 176.
17. *TIME* magazine, Nov. 1, 1993, pg. 49.
18. *The New York Times,* June 9,1990, pg. 8.
19. *American Family Association Newsletter,* Tupelo, Mississippi, pg. 1.
20. Ibid.
21. Ibid.
22. Ibid.
23. Ibid.
24. *Ladies Home Journal,* May, 1990, pg. 103.
25. Ibid. pg. 98.
26. Ibid., pg. 103.
27. Carol Everett, *Selling Teen Abortions,* Easton Publishing Co., Jefferson City, MO. 1992.
28. Ibid.
29. *Los Angeles Times,* May 20,1990, pg. A38.
30. Ibid.
31. *Springfield State Journal-Register,* Nov. 20, 1990
32. Ibid.
33. *PEOPLE* magazine, Aug. 30, 1993, pg. 64.

Chapter 10

1. *PEOPLE* magazine, Nov. 5, 1991, ppg. 53-54.
2. *The Daily Report/Progress Bulletin,* May 29, 1989, pg. A3.
3. Ibid.
4. *Michael Mills Research Ministries Report,* Coldwater, MI, Vol. 1, Issue 1, pg. 2.
5. Ibid.
6. *USA TODAY,* March 5, 1991, ppg. 1-2.

7. *TIME* magazine, Sept. 2, 1991, pg. 60.
8. Article from *Focus on the Family,* Colorado Springs, CO.
9. Ibid.
10. *Family Research Report,* July/Aug. 1992, pg. 3. Quoting the *Colorado Springs Gazette Telegraph,* May 6, 1992.
11. Ibid.
12. Article from *Focus on the Family,* Colorado Springs, CO.
13. Ibid.
14. *No Second Chance,* Video from Jeremiah Films.
15. Ibid.
16. *PARENTS,* May, 1991, pg. 202.
17. *No Second Chance,* Video from Jeremiah Films.
18. *Readers Digest,* August, 1991, pg. 25.
19. *TIME* magazine, Sept. 2, 1991, pg. 60.
20. *Readers Digest,* August, 1991, pg. 25.
21. *PEOPLE* magazine, Nov. 15, 1990, pg. 52.
22. *The New York Times,* June 9,1990, pg. 8.
23. *PEOPLE* magazine, Nov. 15, 1990, pg. 52.
24. *No Second Chance,* Video from Jeremiah Films.
25. *TIME,* September 2, 1991, pg. 60.
26. *AIDS: What You Haven't Been Told,* Video from Jeremiah Films, 1989.
27. *No Second Chance,* Video from Jeremiah Films.
28. *ESSENCE,* June, 1991, ppg. 72-74.
29. *TEEN* Nov., 1993, pg. 43.
30. Ibid.
31. Ibid., pg. 44.

Chapter 11

1. *The Daily Press,* Victorville, CA, Mar. 24, 1991. pg. C-11.
2. Ibid.

3. *Satanism, The Seduction of America's Youth,* ppg. 84,85.

4. Jon Trott, *About The Devil's Business* Cornerstone, Volume 19, Issue 93, pg. 10.

5. *The Arizona Republic,* May 19,1990, pg. C7

6. Ibid. pg. C6.

7. Ibid., pg. C7.

8. *The Daily Press,* Victorville, CA Mar. 9, 1990 pg. A-13.

9. Ibid.

10. Bob Larson, *Satanism, The Seduction of America's Youth,* Nashville, TN, 1989, pg. 86.

11. Ibid.

12. Ibid.

13. Ibid.

14. Ibid., pg. 86.

15. *The Daily Press,* Victorville, CA, June 17, 1990, pg. A-4.

16. Bob Larson, *Satanism, The Seduction of America's Youth,* ppg. 118-119.

17. Ibid., ppg. 103-104.

18. Ibid., pg. 104.

19. *Progress Bulletin,* Apr. 10, 1990, pg. D-1.

20. Ibid.

21. *The Arizona Republic,* May 19,1990, pg. C6.

22. Mark Spaulding, *The Heartbeat of The Dragon,* Light Warrior Press, 1992, pg. 111. Quoting Anton Szandor LaVey, *The Satanic Bible,* Avon Books, 1969, pg. 110.

Chapter 12

1. *Michael Mills Research Ministries Report,* Coldwater, MI, Vol. 1, Issue 1, pg. 18.

2. *Rolling Stone,* June 6, 1985, ppg. 17-18.

3. *USA TODAY,* July 12, 1994, pg. 2D.

4. Mark Spaulding, *The Heartbeat of the Dragon,* Light Warrior Press, 1992, pg. 18.
5. Ibid., pg. 18.
6. Ibid., pg. 50.
7. Ibid., pg. 51.
8. Ibid., pg. 67.

Chapter 13
1. *TIME* magazine, September 2, 1991, pg. 60.
2. *Focus on the Family* magazine, Oct. 1993, Colorado Springs, CO, pg. 5.
3. *Los Angeles Times,* Feb. 27, 1988, Part II, pg. 6.
4. *AIDS: What You Haven't Been Told,* Video from Jeremiah Films
5. Ibid.
6. Ibid.
7. *Christian American,* Feb, 1993, pg. 5.
8. Ibid.
9. *AIDS: What You Haven't Been Told,*
10. Ibid.
11. Ibid.
12. Ibid.
13. Ibid.
14. Ibid.
15. *NFD Journal,* Oct. 1987, pg. 9. (Taken from the *Gay Community News,* Feb. 15-21, 1987.)
16. Ibid., pg. 9.
17. *AIDS: What You Haven't Been Told*
18. *Traditional Values Report,* Vol. 10, No. 2, Nov/Dec. 1991, pg. 6.
19. *No Second Chance,* Video from Jeremiah Films, 1991
20. Ibid.

Chapter 14

1. Rick Jones, *Stairway To Hell*, Chick Pub., 1988, ppg. 89-90.
2. *PEOPLE* magazine, April 25, 1994, pg. 41.
3. *NEWSWEEK* magazine, April 18, 1994, pg. 47.

Chapter 15

1. *Struggling With A Crisis Pregnancy: Four Personal Stories*, 1992, Focus On The Family, Colorado Springs, CO, ppg. 12-14.
2. Ibid.
3. PULPIT HELPS, July, 1994, Pg. 13.
4. *Focus On The Family* Newsletter, July, '93, pg. 4. Quoting from *U.S. Bureau of the Census, Statistical Almanac of the United States:* 1992, 112th edition, Washington, D.C. 1992, pg. 74.
5. *The Challenge To Be Pro-Life*, Cassette tape CS 139, *Focus On The Family*, Colorado Springs, CO.
6. Ibid.
7. Information Brochure FX 308 from Focus On The Family, Colorado Springs, CO, quoting *"Dilation and Extraction for Late Second Trimester Abortion,"* Martin Haskell, M.D., at the National Abortion Federation Risk Management Seminar, September 13-14, 1992, Dallas, Texas.
8. Ibid.
9. Ibid.
10. *Biblical Fundamentalist*, July 15, 1994, pg. 1. (Quoting *Handbook on Abortion*, Dr. and Mrs. J.C. Wilke, Hayes Publishing Co., Cincinnati, OH, 1979, ppg. 89-97.)
11. Focus On The Family Newsletter, Colorado Springs, CO, July, 1993, Pg. 1.
12. Ibid., pg. 2.
13. Biblical Fundamentalist, July 15, 1994, pg. 5.

(Quoting from *Performing Abortions*, Dr. Magda Denes, Commentary, Oct. 1976, ppg. 35,37.

14. Ibid., ppg. 2-4.

15. Ibid., pg. 4. Quoting *"Abortion: Child Sacrifice in the 90's?"* Dr. John D. Currid, Ministry, Summer 1993, Pg. 2

Chapter 16

1. *NEWSWEEK* magazine, Aug. 2, 1993, pg. 40.
2. Ibid., pg. 43.
3. Ibid., pg. 43.
4. *Scholastic Update*, Feb. 11, 1994, pg. 2.
5. Ibid., pg. 8.
6. Ibid., pg. 2
7. Ibid.
8. Ibid., pg. 3.
9. *Los Angeles Times*, June 19,1994, pg. B1.
10. Ibid.
11. Ibid.
12. Newsletter from *Mission Possible, Inc.*
13. *Christian & Society TODAY*, Nov./Dec. 1992, pg. 1.
14. *Scholastic Update*, Feb. 11, 1994, pg. 13.
15. John Muncy, The Role of Rock, Daring Publishing Group, 1989, pg. 266.

ALSO FOR TEENS
BY RICK JONES

This shocking and eye-opening book exposes the step by step plan Satan is using to doom millions of young souls to hell.

Written in simple, easy to read language, it hits teens right where they live. Follow a typical teen as he stumbles, step by step, down the stairway to hell.

ALSO IN SPANISH

Teens will learn where their lifestyle is leading them and discover that Jesus Christ is the *only* way to escape from the stairway to hell. **206 pages, paperback**

More titles by Rick Jones available from CHICK PUBLICATIONS